LOVING YOUR JOB, FINDING YOUR PASSION

Work and the Spiritual Life

Joseph G. Allegretti

PAULIST PRESS
New York/Mahwah, N.J.

Cover design by Tim McKeen

Library of Congress Cataloging-in-Publication Data

Allegretti, Joseph G., 1952-
   Loving your job, finding your passion : work and the spiritual life / Joseph G. Allegretti.
     p. cm.
   Includes bibliographical references.
   ISBN 0-8091-3939-1 (alk. paper)
   1. Work—Religious aspects—Catholic Church. I. Title: Work and the spiritual life. II. Title.
BX1795.W67 A44 2000
248.8'8—dc21   99-087529

Published by Paulist Press
997 Macarthur Boulevard
Mahwah, New Jersey 07430

www.paulistpress.com

Printed and bound in the
United States of America

LOVING YOUR JOB, FINDING YOUR PASSION

CONTENTS

CONTENTS

For My Wife, Suzanne:

Ti Amo

ACKNOWLEDGMENTS

Writing a book is less of a solitary endeavor than commonly supposed. At every step of the way, I have been supported, encouraged, and challenged by other people, many of whom I met face-to-face and others only through their books, letters, phone calls, or e-mails.

I especially want to thank the many people who attended the talks, retreats, and workshops at which the ideas in this book took shape. This is a far better book because of your willingness to share with me your thoughts about work and the spiritual life.

I also want to thank all those who read and commented upon the various drafts of this book, especially my father, Joe Allegretti, who read the manuscript almost as many times as I did. I am indebted to my student assistant, Kristy Collison, for all her hard work. A special word of thanks to Former Dean Larry Raful, Professor Ed Morse, and Professor Ron Volkmer of the Creighton University School of Law for their years of support, encouragement, and friendship. I am grateful to Don Brophy and everyone at Paulist Press for making the editing and publication process so smooth and trouble-free.

Thank you all for your wise counsel. It's not necessary to say it, but I'll say it anyway: I alone am responsible for any defects and omissions.

Above all, I want to thank my family. Once again, my biggest supporters were my two sons, Matt and Pete, and my wife, Suzanne. They remind me each and every day that my work, while important, is not the most important thing in life.

Introduction: Work and the Spiritual Life

It's a Monday evening at a church in the Midwest. A dozen of us have gathered to talk about our work, our values, and our faith.

★ A stay-at-home mother of three sighs, "I spend my whole life changing diapers and cleaning the house. I feel like there's no time for me."

★ "I love my work," says a high school teacher. "I know I'm doing something important with my life."

★ A doctor tells the group, "I worry that my medical practice is taking over my life."

★ A computer programmer complains about the lack of meaning in his job. "I spend eight hours a day punching data into a computer. I'm not doing anything for anyone."

★ A lawyer smiles ruefully and says, "I'm very well paid for what I do, but sometimes I feel more like a prostitute than a professional."

★ "I'll never get rich," says a carpenter, "but I like working with my hands and I like being able to see the results of my work."

During the past few years, I've been meeting with groups of workers interested in exploring the relationship between their spiritual life and their work. Some of our meetings have been at churches, some at retreat centers. Others have been at business offices, schools, law firms, and counseling centers.

Some of the people who attend are devout churchgoers, others are New Age enthusiasts, and many profess no interest in religion at all.

Some love their work; others hate it. Some wake up each morning and can't wait to get to work; others dread the prospect of getting out of bed.

Sales clerks, plumbers, accountants, homemakers, corporate executives, secretaries, dentists, truck drivers, and social workers—the work is infinitely diverse, but the concerns are similar. These people want to feel good about their work. They want it to count for something. They want it to express who they are, their individuality, their values, and their commitments. They don't want to waste their precious days, weeks, months, and years doing empty and meaningless work. They don't want to be one person at home and a different, tougher, meaner person at work.

People want their work to be not only personally satisfying but socially beneficial. They want to feel that their work, in some small way, contributes to the common good and makes this troubled world a better place.

At the same time, people want to achieve a balance between work and home, work and family, work and the rest of life. They want their work to count for something, but they don't want it to take over their whole life. Sure, work is important, but it's not the most important thing in life.

Spirituality Is Not a Four-Letter Word

The people I've met and listened to are only the tip of a great iceberg. There's a deep and growing hunger among people in our society to explore and cultivate a *spirituality of work.*

I hesitate to use the words *spiritual* or *spirituality.* Too often these words conjure up images of monks chanting the psalms, gurus meditating in twisted poses, pious old ladies praying the rosary, sanctimonious charlatans preaching hellfire and brimstone. Many people dismiss spirituality as the very antithesis of the everyday world of work, commerce, and family.

That's why many popular writers reject the term *spiritual* as too otherworldly and prefer to talk about the *soul* or the *soulful life.* They bemoan the "loss of soul" in contemporary society and exhort us to "care for the soul" at work and at home.[1]

But the problem is not with the word *spiritual,* the problem is with us and with our society, which honors only the technological, the scientific, the successful, the productive, the efficient, the consumable—and has no place for the language and the longings of the heart.

Whether we use the word *spirituality,* or the word *soul,* or something else, we are talking about the same thing. The word *spiritual* is a kind of shorthand for the deepest urgings and impulses of the human self. Spirituality is what gives meaning and depth to everyday life. It encompasses our need for creativity, our desire for self-expression, and our hunger for love and for service. Spirituality is the unfolding and the blossoming of the soul.

Spirituality is our way of responding to the mystery at the heart of human experience. Some of us call this dimension God, the sacred, or the divine. Some prefer to talk about a higher power, destiny, or providence. Some call it grace, some call it love.

Call it what you will. Spirituality is our way of experiencing and responding to this ultimate dimension of life. It may take the form of participation in an organized religious tradition, but it doesn't have to. It may be expressed in formal prayer and liturgy, but it doesn't have to. At its core, spirituality is our orientation to the divine, our attentiveness to the holiness of everyday life.

Look at it this way: We all have a spirituality, whether or not we believe in a personal God or attend a church. I often meet people who say, with a hint of pride in their voice, "I'm not religious but I am spiritual." What they say makes perfect sense as long as we understand that spirituality embraces organized religion but isn't limited to it. *Spirituality* is a big word, it encompasses all of life. Think of it this way: *Your spirituality is how you are who you are.*

A Spirituality of Work

Your *spirituality of work* is simply your way of making work a part of your spiritual life. It is how you are who you are *while you are working.*

As you cultivate and nurture a spirituality of work, you will find yourself becoming aware of the opportunities for self-expression in your work. You will come to appreciate the ways in which your work can serve others. You will feel free—free to bring your moral values into the workplace, to stand up for what you believe, to be the same person at work that you are at home and at play.

Most importantly, you will gradually come to realize that all of life is sacred. Moments of grace occur not only in the quiet of a church or the silence of a forest, but amidst the hustle and bustle of a factory floor or the chaos of a busy office. The extraordinary is embedded within the ordinary events of life.

Spirituality is for everyone. A spirituality of work is for everyone, too, for we are all workers. Our language has many words for work. We talk about jobs, careers, occupations, and professions. Government labor statistics carefully distinguish the *em*-ployed from the *un*-employed and report on the plight of the *under*-employed. Society draws a sharp line between workers and retirees. Some people go so far as to claim that only those who get a paycheck are *real* workers, as if staying at home and raising children was a mere avocation, a hobby, for people with nothing else to do!

A spirituality of work should avoid drawing such artificial lines. We all engage in physical and mental labor to perform necessary tasks. Whether we do so for a paycheck is not the point. We all work, and we can all benefit from examining our attitudes toward work. We can all enrich our lives by nurturing the spiritual dimensions of our work.

An Invitation

I invite you to join me in an extended conversation about work and the spiritual life. There are scholars who spend their lives researching sacred tomes, examining exotic spiritual practices, and exploring the mystical dimensions of life. But when it comes to *your* spiritual life, *you* are the only expert. The spiritual journey is for *all* of us, but the path differs for *each* of us.

Our conversation consists of two parts. In part one I explore several ways of talking and thinking about work, including a number of images and metaphors that often influence our approach toward work without our realizing it. As a first step in cultivating a spirituality of work, I examine in some detail the idea of work as a *calling* or *vocation*.

In part two I focus more concretely on a number of steps you can take to make your work more meaningful and to integrate it more fully with your spiritual life. I also examine the perplexing problem of how to achieve a balance between your work and the rest of life.

This book is meant to be a conversation, so feel free to break in at any time, discard what is not helpful, and modify what I say to fit your own needs. If you work at home, for example, you'll want to take my reflections about working in a job outside of the home and adjust them to fit your situation. Each chapter includes a number of exercises and questions. Spend some time doing the exercises and reflecting on the questions. They are designed to let the conversation continue in a way that fits your own situation, lifestyle, and personality. I encourage you to go back to the questions and exercises occasionally, even after you've finished reading the book. Your responses to these questions will undoubtedly change as your life takes you in new and surprising directions.

Think of me not as an expert telling you what to do or how to live, but as a *companion* on your spiritual journey. *Companion* is a beautiful word that comes from the Latin *com-pane:* "with bread." A companion is someone with whom you share bread. I hope that you will see me as your traveling companion, and this book as food for your journey.

Part One:
Exploring
the Language
of Work

WORK IS...

1

The first step in fashioning your own spirituality of work is to become aware of your attitudes toward work. Each of us has our own way of thinking about and understanding work. The easiest way to uncover these assumptions is to take the time to notice the words you habitually use when you talk about work to yourself or to others. Language is the key that can unlock the hidden and usually unconscious images of work that you carry with you.

Let's play a word association game. Before you turn this page, complete the following sentence by jotting down the first few words or phrases that come to mind:

Work is...

Whenever I do this exercise with people, the responses run the gamut. Work is:

Fun
Challenging
Boring
Stressful
Necessary to buy things
Sometimes good and sometimes bad
Unbearable
A career
Important
Exciting
Disappointing
Great
Unavoidable
Creative
Good
Depressing
Easy
Scary
Tedious
Nerve-wracking
Couldn't be better
Spiritual
Frustrating
Invigorating
Lousy
Interesting
Weird
OK
Hard
A waste of time

When you did this exercise, what words came spontaneously to mind? (In the same way, when somebody comes up to you and asks, "How are things going at work?", what's your immediate response before you stop and think about it?)

Notice what the words tell you about your attitudes toward work. Were most of the words you used *positive* (words like *creative, fun, important*)? Did you use *neutral* language (words like *necessary, unavoidable*)? Or did you immediately jot down a laundry list of *negative* words (words like *tedious, depressing, unbearable*)?

Becoming Aware

Most of us possess a number of conflicting images about work, and our language expresses this ambivalence. Our work isn't one thing or the other, but a mix of many things. Sometimes my work is rewarding; sometimes it seems meaningless. Sometimes it's exciting, sometimes tedious. Sometimes I'm invigorated by my work, sometimes I'm depressed by it. During my working life, I've caught myself using *all* of the words listed above. You probably have too.

Go back over your own list and look again at the words you used. Take a particular word that strikes your fancy and reflect upon it for a few moments. What picture or scene comes to mind?

If you jotted down the word *stressful*, for example, close your eyes and say the word silently to yourself. What do you see in your mind's eye? What are you doing? Where are you sitting? Is anyone else present? What are they doing?

If you wrote the word *fun,* stay with that word for a moment. What do you see? What are you doing? Where are you? Are you alone or with others?

By observing our language, we unearth our unconscious assumptions about work. We get a better understanding of what is life-giving and what is death-dealing in our work. And as we bring these unconscious assumptions to consciousness—as we hold them up to the light of day—their power diminishes. They cease to exert an unthinking, automatic influence over us.

The point is *not* to try to change the way you think about your work. It's to become aware of the many different ways you *already* think about your work. As you become aware of this variety, you will also come to realize that some images are more satisfying, more life-giving, and more hopeful than others.

EXERCISES AND QUESTIONS

1. For one week, make a commitment to yourself to pause three or four times a day while working and complete the following sentence:

   At this moment, my work is...

   Each time you do this, jot down the first few words that come to mind. At the end of the week, look back over your answers. What do your answers tell you about your attitudes toward work?

2. Did certain words recur frequently? Did any of the words you wrote down surprise you?

3. Were your responses more positive at certain times of the day or when you were doing certain things? Were there other times of the day when your reactions were mostly negative? What explains the differences in your responses?

4. Notice how other people (friends, family members, colleagues, customers, etc.) talk about their work. Be alert to the words they use to describe their work. What does their language reveal about them? What does it reveal about their attitudes toward work?

5. Now that you are becoming aware of your unconscious attitudes toward work, what's one thing—one simple thing—that you might do differently in the future?

   Now for the tougher questions: Will you do it? Will you make the change or just talk about making it? What's holding you back? Be honest with yourself.

THE (HARD) WORK
OF WORK

2

Our attitudes toward work, of course, must come from somewhere. They're influenced by many factors—our family upbringing, our early work experiences, the media's depiction of various kinds of work (what's glamorous and what's not), our religious tradition, and so on. Among the most important influences are the general understandings of work in our society. Our attitudes toward work can't help but be shaped by these cultural understandings—they are like the air we breathe, invisible, yet inescapable, surrounding us at every moment. The ambivalence that most of us feel about our work reflects the varying and even contradictory meanings of work that hold sway in our society.

*   *   *

Let's begin with the simplest and most basic understanding of work. *Work* is often defined as an "activity in which someone uses physical or mental effort to do something." Work is the use of our minds or bodies to accomplish something.

If we look at it this way, almost everything we do is work! Making dinner, cleaning the house, going shopping, mowing the lawn—all are work. So is playing chess, making a quilt, bowling, or tinkering with the car.

This definition is so broad that it might seem meaningless, but it does serve to remind us of an important point:

> *Work cannot be divorced from physical and mental exertion!*

Work can be creative, meaningful, and fun, but we delude ourselves if we think that it will ever stop being work.

Sometimes we fantasize about finding the "perfect" job—a job of a certain kind, in a certain city, with a certain salary. We tell ourselves: If only I had a better job, I'd be happy. I'd be satisfied with my life. I'd be a better husband or wife....

Finding the "right" work *is* an important goal, well worth pursuing, and I'll have a lot to say about it throughout this book. But while the right work can bring a person joy and contentment, it's a delusion to think that the right work will be easy or effortless. No work is without effort. As its root meaning indicates, work, even (especially?) work you love, is *hard work*. I can attest to this as I write these words on my computer; I love to write, but I'd be a liar if I said it was easy.

Other common definitions of work underscore this point. My dictionary includes the following synonyms for *work: labor, travail, toil, drudgery,* and *grind.* Each of these words emphasizes the idea of work as involving effort and exertion. As we move through the list, in fact, the meanings become more and more negative. *Drudgery* refers to dull, monotonous work; *grind* to work that is exhausting to the mind or body. But even the most neutral of these words, *labor,* is defined as "physical or mental exertion."

A Dose of Reality

No matter how much you like your work, there are times when it's difficult, mornings when it's hard to drag yourself out of bed, days when the office or the factory feels more like punishment than paradise. If you think of your work unrealistically, and hold expectations that it can't satisfy, you're setting yourself up for disappointment. No work or job will be good enough. You'll always feel like a scorned lover who was promised so much but given so little.

We've all known people like this, people who seem congenitally unable to stay in a job for more than a few months. They start with high hopes but become disillusioned as soon as reality sets in—which doesn't take long. Once their dream is shattered, they flee for greener pastures. They spend their entire life flitting from job to job in a vain quest to capture the Holy Grail of the workplace, the once-and-future job that will satisfy all their needs and desires.

Then there are the perennially discontented workers who *should* leave their jobs but don't. These people hate what they do, but rather than move on, they stay put, burrow into their work like moles, and end up making the workplace a living hell for everyone around them. These are the people who, once disillusioned, can't find a single good thing to say about their work. They despise their boss. Their office chair hurts their back. Their colleagues are all hypocrites. They aren't being paid what they deserve. The water in the cooler has a funny taste. Since their work can't satisfy them completely (what could?), they convince themselves that it can't satisfy them at all.

Both of these groups—those who can't stay put in a job and those who shouldn't—share the same problem. *They do not recognize work for what it is.* They expect too much from it. You can avoid these extremes by adopting a realistic view of your work. Work can be many things: a source of personal meaning, an expression of your creativity, a vehicle for service, an element in your spiritual journey. It can be all these things and more. But whatever it is, your work will always be work.

EXERCISES AND QUESTIONS

1. How realistic are you about your work? Is the grass always greener at another office or factory? Have you switched jobs often?

2. Do you sometimes fantasize about finding the "perfect" work? Try this exercise: Sit down in a comfortable chair, close your eyes, and imagine what your perfect job would look like.

   Be concrete. Where are you (in an office, on a beach, in a kitchen, on a space station)? What do your surroundings look like (artwork on the walls, music in the background)? What are you doing (singing, talking, welding, sleeping)? What are the benefits of the job (good salary, nice colleagues, a Jacuzzi in the office)? Spend some time playing with whatever images come to mind.

3. Now ask yourself: What am I willing to do to make this fantasy come true? Be honest. If your answer is *not much,* then your fantasy might be getting in the way of reality. It might be blocking you from seeing the opportunities for growth and success in your present work. If, on the other hand, you're already working to make your dream come true (maybe you dream of being a famous actor and you're taking a drama class), don't be too quick to discard it as unrealistic.

4. When someone asks you how your work is going, what's your immediate response? How much time and energy do you spend complaining and whining about your work? Does any of your negative

talk lead to something positive? Do you ever (often, occasionally, once a decade) have anything good to say about your work?

5. What's one thing you like about your present work or job? (Admit it, there must be *something*.) Write it down on a sheet of paper, stick it in your pocket, and look at it the next time things are going badly.

WHEN WORK IS A JOB

3

At its most basic, work is a form of mental or physical activity, but most of us don't think of our work that way. When we talk about the *workday,* the *workweek,* the *workforce,* and the *worker,* we're referring to a certain kind of activity—to work as the *means by which we make a living.* When we talk about our work, we mean our job.

This meaning of work relates closely to the word *employment.* Someone who works for herself is *self*-employed, someone who can't find work is *un*-employed, and someone who has a job that doesn't fully utilize her talents is *under*-employed.

Most of us—at least those with a paid job—can't help but think about our work this way. If someone asks, "What do you do?", we tell them about our job. If someone asks, "Where do you work?", we give them the name of our employer.

Although this is a common way of talking and thinking about work, it presents certain risks. First, and most obviously, it can make us forget that a lot of work isn't paid work. A woman raising two young children is certainly working, even if she isn't employed outside of the home. And even for those of us who do get a paycheck, our work doesn't end the moment we punch a time clock or lock up the office. Cleaning diapers, making dinner, doing laundry, mowing the lawn—all these are definitely work. If we want to explore the spiritual significance of our work, we shouldn't ignore these activities just because they don't carry a paycheck.

The Inner Meaning of Work

There's another, more subtle, problem with thinking about work only as a job done for pay. You might fool yourself into believing that your work is important only for the money or the benefits it can bring, not for anything inherent in what you do.

If you see your work as a job and only a job, then it's nothing but a way to earn a living, a means to an end. When you approach your work this way, however, it goes flat, losing its zest and vitality. It becomes an Italian meal without (God forbid!) the oil and the garlic. You might not hate your work, but you certainly don't love it—you just do it. You show up on time, put in your eight (or nine or ten) hours, do what you have to do, and escape as soon as you can.

As theologian Frederick Buechner reminds us:

> Jobs are what people do for a living, many of them for eight hours a day, five days a week, minus vacations, for most of their lives. It is tragic to think of how few of them have their hearts in it. They work mainly for the purpose of making money enough to enjoy their moments of not working.[1]

When you treat your work this way, it has no *inner meaning,* no meaning in and of itself. Your work loses its capacity to nourish you spiritually. There's no place left in it for beauty, wonder, and love. It can't provide the sense of creativity and service that you crave. Instead, when you go to work you feel as if you've left a part of yourself at home—the best part, the deepest part, the real part.

More Than a Job

In his book, *Working,* Studs Terkel talks of the "happy few who find a savor in their daily jobs; the Indiana stonemason, who looks upon his work and sees that it is good; the Chicago piano tuner, who seeks and finds the sound that delights; the bookbinder, who saves a piece of history; the Brooklyn firefighter, who saves a piece of life."

What is the common bond among these lucky people who find satisfaction and fulfillment in their work? According to Terkel, these people find "a meaning in their work well over and beyond the reward of the paycheck."[2] *They see their work as a job, but more than a job.*

I've experienced this in my work, not all the time, but sometimes. Sometimes, although I'm working hard, it doesn't seem like work—the hours fly by like minutes, and I'm refreshed rather than exhausted by my efforts. I feel good about what I'm doing and good about myself. My work expresses my creativity. It gives me a sense of purpose and a way to serve the larger community. There's no longer any gap between my work and my personal and spiritual values; my life is integrated rather than divided. At these times, my work is important over and above the paycheck it provides.

I said earlier that you need to be realistic about your work. You shouldn't forget that work is work (and often hard work at that). That's good advice. At the same time, however, if you want to be *really* realistic about your work, you need to recognize that it can also be spiritually enriching and enlivening, if you let it.

I'll return to this theme later and at greater length. For now, however, what's important is for you to become aware of the ways in which you think and talk about your work. Do you treat it only as a job, or as something more, something better?

If you find yourself treating your work as only a job (and most of us do, sometimes), remind yourself that such a cramped notion of work doesn't do justice to the opportunities it can offer you. It doesn't do justice to you, either. Your work is more than a job—and you are more, much more, than a worker.

EXERCISES AND QUESTIONS

1. Complete this sentence:

   I work to...

   Don't just write down one or two words. That's much too easy. Write down *all* the reasons you work. Not only the obvious ones (to make money, provide for your kids, etc.). Include all your reasons, no matter how unimportant they seem (to get out of the house, have an excuse to dress up, etc.).

2. What does your list tell you about yourself? Are there any surprises? Looking at my list, I realize that most of my reasons for working have nothing to do with making money, but with finding meaning and satisfaction. On the other hand, I did write down "earn a living" first....

3. Are there times—there must be—when your work seems to lack meaning in and of itself but is only a way to make a living? Think back to the last time you experienced one of these dry spells. How long did it last? What kept you going? What brought you out of it and restored a sense of meaning to your work?

4. Now think back to a time when your work was more than a job—when you experienced a sense of meaning, fulfillment, and creativity in your work. What were you doing? How long did the feeling last? What caused it to fade?

5. Can you put your finger on the reasons why your work seems to lack inner meaning at some times yet be full of meaning at other times? What's the difference? What are you doing differently?

6. What can you do to cultivate that elusive "something more" that makes your work personally satisfying and spiritually enriching? Try to be concrete. What's one thing that you could do right now to make your work more than a job?

   Once again, be honest with yourself. It's better to do one small thing than dream of doing many great things.

CURSED BE
THE GROUND

4

It's a small step from treating your work as devoid of spiritual meaning (Oh well, it's just a job. Yawn...) to treating it as something different, something worse, something destructive of your spiritual life—not a job but a *curse*.

This is the dark vision of work that Studs Terkel expresses at the beginning of his book *Working*:

> This book, being about work, is, by its very nature about violence—to the spirit as well as the body. It is about ulcers as well as accidents, about shouting matches as well as fistfights, about nervous breakdowns as well as kicking the dog around. It is, above all (or beneath all) about daily humiliations. To survive the day is triumph enough for the walking wounded among the great many of us.[1]

Work is about violence. It is about humiliation. Survival is the only victory.

Many people feel this way. They may earn large salaries and live in the nicest of neighborhoods. Yet their work is nothing but a grim necessity—it provides no sustenance for their souls, no bread for their spiritual journey. Often their faces brighten up—lighten up!—the moment the conversation shifts from work to what's really important in their lives, whether it's family, friends, church, or hobbies.

★ "I hate what I do but I have no choice. I've got to earn money for my family," a postal worker tells me.

★ "It pays well, so I do it, but it leaves a bad taste in my mouth," says a successful corporate lawyer.

★ A young man who works in his family's business says, "I always wanted to be a writer, but the only things I write are office memos. Someday I'll be the boss here, and I could care less."

★ A woman who works in an insurance company says, "It takes all my energy just to make it through the day. Sometimes, tears well up in my eyes for no reason. I dream about jumping in my car and taking off somewhere, anywhere, by myself."

Hate Your Work, Hate Yourself

The worst thing about hating your work is the effect upon yourself. If you think of your work as a curse, it diminishes your own value. Here you are, spending hour after hour, day after day, month after month, year after year, engaged in aimless and hollow activity that is irrelevant to the deepest yearnings of your heart and soul. What does this say about you? What kind of person must you be to squander your life doing meaningless work?

You may end up hating yourself for wasting your life. Of course, you might not admit this to yourself.

Most of us are skilled in the art of self-deception. But when you refuse to face it, your self-loathing doesn't disappear. It sinks below the surface and reemerges in disguised form, perhaps as self-destructive behavior such as drug or alcohol abuse. You may eat too much, drink too much, spend too much, party too hardy, all in a futile effort to escape that nagging sense of self-hatred that won't let you go. Self-abuse is almost always a telltale sign of self-hatred turned into self-punishment.

It may seem that I'm overstating the problem. Not all of us hate our work or hate ourselves for what we do at work. Some of us love what we do. Some people, of course, are better equipped to find meaning and fulfillment in their work than others. Some see the glass half full, some see it half empty (and some have a hard time seeing any water at all). These differences are rooted in our personality, our upbringing, or even our genes.

All of us, however, go through periods when our work is dry and lifeless. All of us have found ourselves hating what we do. All of us have dreamt of winning the lottery and never having to work again. To that extent, all of us struggle with the temptation to see our work as a curse without meaning.

By the Sweat of Your Brow

Ironically, people who are more spiritually attentive, more committed to the spiritual path, are *more likely* than other people to treat their work as a curse. How can this be? It is because spirituality in the West has typically been thought of as something distinct from and even antithetical to ordinary life and work. In the Book of Genesis, for example, God tells Adam and Eve:

> Cursed be the ground because of you;
> By toil shall you eat of it
> All the days of your life:
> Thorns and thistles shall it sprout for you.
> But your food shall be the grasses of the field;
> By the sweat of your brow
> Shall you get bread to eat....[2]

Work, back-breaking, mind-numbing work is depicted as God's punishment for the primeval, original sin of humanity. (The Bible also contains other, more positive accounts of work, but it's the negative picture that sticks in people's minds.) I can still recall listening as a child to sermons on this passage. The message could not have been clearer: Work is tough, and that's tough luck, for work is laid under a curse from God!

More subtly, religion has often encouraged the mistaken notion that God and the spiritual life are reserved for Sundays and holy days—which has the effect of trivializing the value of everyday life and work. Too often, spirituality in the West has been thought of as something you can do only if you escape from ordinary life, not immerse yourself in it.

In the Middle Ages, for example, it was often assumed that no one who remained in the secular world could live out the fullness of the Christian faith. Those who worked, married, and raised families were relegated to second-class citizenship in the kingdom of God.

Scholars are quick to point out that the Protestant Reformation shattered the medieval worldview by insisting that there was no real distinction between a sacred "calling" and secular work. No longer was secular work second best.

The scholars may be right, but I wonder....Don't the remnants of the medieval view haunt us still? Don't we still make a sharp distinction between our work and our spiritual life? If you go on a retreat, sit quietly in a church, read an inspirational book, meditate in private, take a walk in the forest—that is considered spiritual. But the rest of your life, the time spent at work, with the kids, fixing dinner, cleaning clothes, rushing to the supermarket or the veterinarian—that is usually thought of as secular, profane, anything but spiritual.

From such a viewpoint, the long hours we spend at work are at best a waste of time, and at worst a cause of spiritual guilt and anxiety. Work distracts us from our real purpose in life—to deepen our relationship with God. No wonder so many people treat their work as a curse!

The cure for this split between the sacred and the profane isn't to quit your job and become a religious hermit. The cure lies in seeing your life and work in a different way. The spiritual life encompasses everything you do. Time spent at work is no less important and no less spiritual than time spent in prayer or meditation. Your work doesn't have to be a curse—it becomes a curse only when you choose to curse it.

EXERCISES AND QUESTIONS

1. Look back to the quotation from Studs Terkel at the beginning of the chapter. To what extent do you agree with his assessment? To what extent is your work about violence and humiliation? Be honest.

2. Think back to the last occasion when you treated your work as a curse. What brought on the attitude? How did it start? How long did it last? Is there a certain situation or pattern of events (every time the quarterly report is due, every time you have to leave town on business, etc.) that usually brings on these negative feelings?

3. Think back again to the last occasion when your work seemed utterly meaningless. What was the effect on the rest of your life? Did you eat too much? Drink too much? Watch too much TV? Suffer from nagging stomach or back pains? Mope around the house? Pick fights with your family or friends?

4. What helps to dissolve these feelings of meaningless? Be specific. What works for you (talking to a friend, praying, laughing, taking a day off, etc.)?

5. Complete the following sentence:

The next time I find myself treating work as a curse I will...

Come back to this the next time you find yourself cursing your work.

6. Do you have a tendency to think of your work as separate from or even opposed to your spiritual life? When you hear the words *spiritual,* or *spirituality,* what comes to mind?

CLIMBING THE LADDER OF SUCCESS

5

Work can be a job and sometimes it can be a curse. But there are other words that suggest a deeper, even spiritual, dimension to our work. Work can be *career*, it can be a *profession,* and maybe it can even be a *calling.*

Consider the word *career*. A "career" is usually defined as *one's chosen work over the course of a lifetime.* We talk of a military career or a diplomatic career. Closer to home, a person who dedicates herself to a particular line of work is said to have a career—she might pursue a career in nursing, engineering, or banking.

Career implies a series of steps, a path, or a ladder that leads gradually to more important and prestigious assignments. An employee who puts in long years with one company, rising slowly from a basement cubicle to a corporate penthouse suite, is said to have had a successful career.

It's helpful to contrast the idea of a career with a job. As we saw earlier, a job is merely a way to earn a living. Your success in a job is measured by the size of your paycheck. But in a career, says Robert Bellah, success is "defined by a broader sort of success, which takes in social standing and prestige, and by a sense of expanding power and competency that renders work itself a source of self-esteem."[1]

If you have a career, your work becomes a way to accomplish something worthwhile with your life. It's a source of self-fulfillment. It nourishes your self-esteem. Your work has meaning in and of itself.

When you see your work as a career, you commit yourself to a long period of learning, training, and maturing. Little by little, year by year, you gradually acquire greater experience and skills, assume greater responsibilities, and obtain greater rewards. In a career, you're in it for the long haul.

This way of thinking about a career is positive, but the word has some negative connotations as well. These hint at the risks associated with approaching your work this way.

From Career to Careerism

The word *career* comes from the Latin word for *road,* and, before that, for *vehicle.* One of its older meanings was to go at full speed, which suggests that a career can get out of hand. The constant striving for success can throw your entire life out of kilter. Your career can *run away* with you, making you feel as if you're in an automobile hurtling down a mountain road without any brakes. When this happens, you might catch yourself muttering to yourself, "I've got to slow down! My life is out of control!"

If we look at a dictionary, the next word after career is *careerism,* which suggests that it's only a short step from the former to the latter. *Careerism* is the practice of *using all possible means to advance your career, moral or otherwise.* If you treat your work as a career and concentrate on climbing the ladder of success, it becomes easy to lose sight of the moral consequences of your actions. If career advancement is your one and only goal, then anything goes! Nothing can be allowed to get in the way of success.

We catch a hint of this meaning in the way we sometimes talk about a "career bank robber" or a "career criminal." The cutthroat salesperson, the army general who covers-up wrongdoing, the politician who employs spin-doctors to massage and distort the truth, the business executive who decides it's cheaper to market a dangerous product than to test it first—these are commonplace examples of people whose zeal for a career has degenerated into immoral careerism. They are like the hired guns of the Wild West who would do anything, shoot anyone, as long as their work called for it.

There's another risk, too. If I invest too much of myself in my career, success becomes more and more elusive. It's not enough to have a good job with good pay. No, I must have a great job with great pay. It's not enough to rise to a position of authority in my company. No, I must rise to the top, the very top. Anything less than total success is failure.

This struck home for me when I attended a retirement party for a family friend who had served as the number-two executive at a medium-sized company. I congratulated him on his accomplishments, but he waved them aside. Instead, he spoke bitterly about how unfairly he had been treated by the company—how he had deserved to be the boss but was outmaneuvered by a young upstart. Here was a man who had spent forty years with one company, climbing as far up the corporate ladder as anyone could hope, yet he felt like a failure because he was ending his career one rung from the top.

A career is not enough. It's not enough to do *well* at work. It's not enough to climb the ladder of success. For your work to be spiritually enriching, it has to be *good* work. It has to be work that expresses who you are, makes the world a better place, and satisfies the soul instead of just the ego.

Too many people claw and climb their way to the top, only to find that it wasn't worth the effort. When they finally make it to the top of the ladder of success, they discover that it's leaning against the wrong wall.

EXERCISES AND QUESTIONS

1. What does the word *career* mean to you? Do you think of yourself as having a career? Why or why not?

2. Regardless of whether you think of yourself as having a career, would you like to have one? Why? What are the major benefits of having a career? Be specific.

3. What are the drawbacks to a career? Is there anything about the idea of a career that troubles you or scares you? Be specific.

4. Have you ever been on a career path and left it? Why? Looking back, did you do the right thing?

5. If you *don't* think of yourself as having a career, complete the following sentence:

   In order to have a career, I would have to commit myself to...

6. If you do think of yourself as having a career, complete the following sentence:

   In order to achieve my career, I have been willing to...

   Now ask yourself: Has it been worth it? Have the benefits been worth the costs?

7. Is it possible to have a successful career but waste your life? Have you known anyone like this? Is there a lesson here for you?

WHAT WORK
PROFESSES

6

The word *career* invites you to think of your work as more than a job. The word *profession* invites you to take a further step and situate your work within a wider frame of meaning. While the idea of a career has little if anything to do with helping others (remember the example of the career criminal), the notion of a profession is rooted in an ideal of service to the community.

The word *profession* comes originally from the Latin, meaning *to profess openly*. In the early Middle Ages, the word was used to refer to the taking of religious vows. We still use the word in this sense when we talk of the vows made by a monk or a nun upon entering a religious order. Over time, the word came to mean any kind of particularly solemn promise or declaration ("I profess my love for you").

By the late Middle Ages, the word was used to refer to occupations—such as law, medicine, and ministry—which required specialized knowledge, long years of academic preparation, and high ideals. The older idea of a vow wasn't lost entirely. When a young man (it would be hundreds of years before a young woman could enter a profession) was about to become a doctor or a lawyer, he had to profess his commitment to the ideals of his chosen field. An aspiring doctor professed to cure and not to kill, while the would-be lawyer professed to serve justice.[1]

The idea of a profession, then, includes a commitment to service rather than self-interest, to the good of the community rather than personal gain. Professionals dedicate—profess—themselves to serving this higher good.

At least that's what they tell us...

The Good, the Bad, the Professional

Today, our view of the professions is decidedly ambivalent. On the one hand, there's been a great expansion of the concept. No longer are the professions limited to law, medicine, and ministry. Nurses, accountants, and engineers consider themselves professionals and are considered so by society.

But the expansion doesn't stop there. Look at the classified section of your newspaper, under the listings for "professionals," and you'll find a bewildering profusion of jobs: movers and carpenters, teachers and customer service representatives, dental hygienists and massage therapists. Doctors are professionals; so are drywallers. It seems as if almost everyone is—or wants to be—a professional.

There are a number of reasons for this expansion. Some people hope to use the title to project an image of dedication and competence. Some count on it to bring them greater prestige and autonomy.

(Who wants to be a "truck driver" when you can be a "professional driver"? Why call yourself a "painter" when you can advertise as a "professional painting service"?) And many believe that as professionals they'll be able to get away with charging exorbitant fees.

Yet along with this expansion of the professions, we've also witnessed a decline in trust and respect for professionals. No longer are they seen as wonder-workers who inhabit an exalted realm above mere mortals and who must be obeyed without question. Lawyers are the butt of nasty jokes about their avarice and immorality, doctors are distrusted for their greed and paternalism, and even the clergy have come in for criticism aimed at their hypocrisy and narrow-mindedness.

A Commitment to Service

What are we to make of this? Sociologists often try to identify the characteristics that distinguish "true" professions from imposters. For our purposes, it's more important to focus on the original and underlying meaning of the word.

The history of the word suggests that any kind of work can be a profession, if it's performed solemnly, with a commitment to serving ends greater than your own. A dedication to something *bigger than yourself* is the hallmark of a profession.

Whether you're a sales clerk, a trucker, a computer programmer, a teacher, a dentist, a beautician, a journalist—no matter what your work, you have the opportunity to contribute to the welfare of the community. As soon as you recognize this, your work ceases to be just a job. It becomes a kind of profession about who you are and how you choose to use your talents. It becomes a way—not the only way, of course, but a way—to express your deepest needs to love and to serve. Your work becomes a spiritual practice.

Approaching your work this way can help protect you against the temptation toward careerism. As we saw in the last chapter, the idea of a career can be a good thing if it encourages you to develop your talents and accomplish something worthwhile. But if your career degenerates into careerism, the result is amorality and spiritual stagnation. At its best, the idea of a profession functions as a check upon careerism by reminding you that your work is a means of serving others, not just your own interests. It forces you to ask: Why am I doing this? Who benefits from it?

I'm certainly not suggesting that all professionals (or workers in general) live up to these high ideals. Think back to the last time you visited a doctor: Did you feel that the doctor was there to serve you? That your interests came first?

When I'm a patient, I show up at the office when I'm told, undergo whatever tests the doctor orders, and listen dumbly while the doctor "explains" my condition using medical gobbledygook I can't understand. I usually have only the vaguest idea of what's wrong with me or why I'm doing what I'm doing. Too often I feel as if I'm there to serve the doctor, not the other way around.

Professions exist to serve the public, but some professionals profess little more than a commitment to serving themselves and their own interests. It's easy for a professional (or for any worker who aspires to be treated like a professional), to think of himself as better than the person he's hired to serve. It's tempting to shift the focus from helping others to helping himself. To substitute selfishness for selflessness.

Given these risks, it's not enough for us to approach our work as a profession. Perhaps it would be better if each of us put less emphasis on what we *profess* to be doing with our work, and more emphasis on what we are *called* to do with our work. Less emphasis on *what* we do and more on *how* we do it.

Perhaps a spirituality of work requires a little more listening and a little less professing.

EXERCISES AND QUESTIONS

1. Are you most likely to think of your work as:

   a. A job.
   b. A career.
   c. A profession.

2. Why did you answer the way you did? Be specific. What do you like and what do you dislike about each of these ways of looking at your work?

3. What does your work say about you? Put it another way: What do you *profess* about yourself by your work and the way you do it? What would you like other people to say about you and the work you do?

4. How is your work an instrument of service? How does it help other people? If you draw a blank, broaden your imagination: A payroll clerk makes sure employees get the pay they've earned; an air conditioner repair person helps people stay comfortable in hot weather; a department store clerk helps customers find clothes they need and can afford; a worker with children at home is putting food on the table and a roof over her family's head, whatever kind of work she is doing.

5. Do you have a job that tempts you to think of yourself as better or more important than the people you serve? Be honest now! If you're a doctor, lawyer, banker, or corporate big shot—if you've got the kind of job that pays well and brings lots

of perks and status—then the odds are that your
answer will be *yes*.

6. If your job tempts you to think of yourself as better than other people, what can you do to stop
them from putting you on a pedestal? Are you willing to step down from the pedestal and treat other
people as your equal? Are you willing to serve
rather than be served? What's stopping you?

THE GOD WHO CAN'T SAVE

7

If you treat your work as a *career* or a *profession,* you run the risk of investing too much of yourself in your work. Instead of treating your work as a curse, without meaning, you might end up doing just the opposite and treat it as something more than it is—something great, something almost godlike.

Theologian James Dittes makes the point well:

> [Our] most intense religious commitment is often to work. We give it absolute devotion, we expect our work to save us, to make us feel whole and healthy and right, cured from the gnawing sense that there is something wrong with us. Sometimes it does this, for awhile. But often the sacramental powers of work become crumbled idols, and we find ourselves religiously dedicated to a god unworthy of our ardor, trusting a god unable to deliver a saving.[1]

Idolatry is confusing the finite with the infinite. An idol doesn't have to be a carved statue or a hunk of bone—an idol is any god unworthy of our adoration, any god unable to deliver salvation. Our god is whoever or whatever assumes ultimate significance in our life, whoever or whatever is the fixed point around which the rest of our life revolves. When we give our work too much significance, we make it our god.

Worshiping Work

Work idolatry is an occupational hazard for many workers, but especially so for those who convince themselves they're doing "important" work. Many doctors, lawyers, and business executives, for example, are overachievers, workaholics, who place inflated value upon their work. For many of these people, work is their entire life. Everything else suffers—families and friends fall by the wayside, cherished hobbies are forgotten, their own health is jeopardized—in their frantic efforts to work more, do more, earn more.

I've met many "successful" professionals and business executives who spend so much time at the office that it has become their surrogate home. I've listened to a top salesman tell me that his only friends were his clients, because only with his clients did he feel really alive and productive. I've been told by a prominent banker, "When I got married, I told my wife that the job came first!" He hadn't been kidding, he said with a wry grin, because he'd said the same thing to his next three wives, too.

You've known people like this. Maybe you've felt the temptation yourself. The physician whose private life is a shambles and who compensates by throwing herself into her work. The young corporate whiz kid who can find nothing to fill up his empty evenings except more hours at the office and more projects to begin. The hard-working, hard-drinking journalist who lives and eats and drinks to excess, only to drop dead of a heart attack at forty.

The broken marriages, the drug and alcohol problems, the push-push-push mentality that can never slow down or ease up—these are the telltale signs of the idolatrous worship of the god of work.

How often I fall into this trap! Even when I'm busy at work, with lots to do, I find myself saying *yes* to each new project, never *no*, trying not only to complete them all but complete them all *perfectly*, as if anything less would be utter failure. How tempting it is as a teacher to delude myself into thinking that one more lecture, one more article, will make me feel good about myself. It's as if there's a yawning pit in my life, a hollow center, greedily demanding to be filled up by my work and accomplishments.

But each success only brings new challenges and anxieties. No matter what I achieve there's always the lingering fear that next time I won't be so lucky, next time I'll fail. That's the problem with the god of work—no matter what you do, it's never enough.

The Paradox of Work

There's a paradox here that cuts to the very heart of an authentic spirituality of work: Work should be taken seriously. It's an important part of the spiritual life. But it's not of *ultimate* significance. Work should open us to the spiritual and the divine, not become our god.

We have to be careful not to let our work become the chief test of our self-worth. It's easy to confuse *who I am* with *what I do*. Work can become our way of shouting to the world (and to ourself), "Look at me, I'm good, I count for something!"

When this happens, we're not working to live—we're living to work. Without our work what's left? I think of the elderly man who told me, "All my life I've been an engineer. Now that I'm retired I'm nothing."

Our society contributes to this way of thinking. At a cocktail party, we break the ice with strangers by asking, "What do you do? Where do you work?" The size of our paycheck or our office serves as a not-too-subtle sign of divine favor, proof that we're some-body special, somebody important. And woe to the unemployed and underemployed in a culture like ours that enshrines work, accomplishment, and pro-ductivity as the chief tests of a person's value!

There's no quick fix for this problem, but a first step is to admit our tendency toward work idolatry. That's a fact of life for most of us, to a greater or lesser extent, because our work *does* matter. It makes a dif-ference if we do it well or do it poorly. If it didn't make a difference, we'd be treating it as a curse.

So let's admit that our work is important and is inextricably entangled with our self-image. Problems arise not when our work is meaningful but when it assumes *ultimate meaning* in our lives, when we try to use it to win salvation. That's too much to expect from our work, and deep down we know it.

Deep down we know that nothing outside of ourself—no job or car or luxury condo—can save us. Things can't deliver salvation. Work can't make everything better. It can't compensate for failed relationships, shadowy fears, and lifelong insecurities. True salvation has to come from within, from the divine spark that exists in each of us.

The real risk is that we might end up like the man whose gravestone was spotted in a Scottish cemetery:

Here lies John McDonald
Born a Man
Died a Grocer[2]

It's a good thing to be a grocer. It's honorable work that serves the common good. If John McDonald's epitaph was intended to memorialize his pride in a job well done, we can understand and applaud it.

But I wonder...is it really possible to look at a man's life—his loves and hates, his laughter and tears, his successes and failures, his hopes and dreams—and compress and condense it all into a few words about work? Is that all there is? Doesn't it diminish the wonder and the mystery of his life—and all our lives?

Born a man, born a woman—but died a grocer, a dentist, a priest, or a painter, as if work and work alone gave meaning and purpose to life.

The paradoxical nature of work calls for a paradoxical solution. Let's look for meaning in our work, but not too much meaning. Let's take it seriously, but not too seriously. Let's appreciate it, but not worship it. If there's an answer to the paradox of work, it lies somewhere between damning our work as a curse and worshiping it as an idol.

EXERCISES AND QUESTIONS

1. Close your eyes and picture yourself. What do you see? Where are you? What are you doing?

2. Take a sheet of paper and complete this sentence:

   The five most important things in my life are:
   First...
   Second...
   Third...
   Fourth...
   Fifth...

3. Now, complete the following sentence:

   The five things I spend the most time doing are:
   First...
   Second...
   Third...
   Fourth...
   Fifth...

4. Do your two lists match? What can you learn from comparing them? Very few people admit that work is the most important thing in their life. But many of us spend a lot more time working than we do on other things that we claim are more important, like our family, our friends, or our relationship with God.

5. Review a typical week (if you have an appointment calendar, use it to jog your memory). How many hours a week do you spend working at a job for pay? How many hours do you spend doing

unpaid work? How many hours do you spend getting ready for work, going to and from work, cleaning up after work, and so forth? How many hours do you spend thinking about work, worrying about work, checking your voice mail, etc.?

6. Think back to your last vacation. Did you bring work with you? How much time did you spend working and worrying about work? (If you can't remember the last time you had a vacation, I trust you get the point!) Do you sometimes do work on weekends that could wait until the workweek?

7. If you're investing too much time and energy in your work, ask yourself: Has work become an escape from the rest of my life? Would I rather be working than not working? Be honest with yourself.

8. All of us want to do well at work, but how do you react when things don't go well? How do you handle disappointments? Do failures at work make you feel like a failure as a person?

THE CALL OF WORK

8

Whether we think of our work as a *job*, a *career*, or even a *profession*, our spiritual life suffers. We end up treating our work as nothing but a *curse*. Or, in a misguided effort to compensate, we turn it into an *idol*.

Clearly, we need to find other images of work that aren't so limited, images that are creative, fertile, and life-giving. We need an approach to work that's *positive* but not *too positive*—an approach that holds to the middle course and neither reduces work to a devil nor elevates it to a god.

What are these positive images and attitudes? Where do we find them?

When people share with me their healthy visions of work and when I find myself spiritually enriched and invigorated by my work, the term that seems to express what is happening is the religious word *calling* (or *vocation;* they mean the same).

The word *vocation* comes from the Latin word for a call or summons. The dictionary speaks of a vocation as a "summons or strong inclination toward a certain kind of work," especially the religious life. It can also be defined as "a strong feeling that God has called you to a particular line of work." A vocation is something you have to listen for and respond to.

Profession or Vocation?

It's interesting to compare the meanings of the words *profession* and *vocation* in today's society. As we saw earlier, there's a mystique surrounding the word *profession*—lots of people call themselves professionals to imply competence and justify charging high fees. On the other hand, the word *vocation* is used today for jobs that are technical, manual, and command little status. If you don't go to college, you might go to vocational school to learn a trade like plumbing or mechanics.

Throughout much of history, however, *vocation* had the higher, more exalted status. In the Middle Ages, for example, vocation specifically meant a religious calling—the call to ministry in the church. Only those who renounced the secular world to serve God were said to have a calling.

Some of us still cling to these older notions. I attended parochial school in the 1960s, my children in the 1990s. Much has changed over the past thirty years, but one thing has not—when my children's school hosts its annual "vocations day," nuns and priests and an occasional monk come and talk about their work. Carpenters, bankers, and secretaries do not.

This old-fashioned idea of *calling* encourages us to draw a rigid line between the sacred and the profane dimensions of our life. It contributes to the delusion that our everyday work lacks spiritual significance.

A New View of Calling

The medieval church was right to affirm the sanctity of work, but wrong to claim that only *some* jobs, religious jobs, constituted a calling. This was recognized in the 1500s by the Protestant Reformers, thinkers like Martin Luther and John Calvin, who taught that any work could be approached as a calling. In Luther's theology, for example, "[a]ny occupation becomes a 'calling' if its primary motive is serving God, responding to God's wishes and intentions for human existence....Our vocation becomes that of loving the neighbor through our occupation."[1] From this point of view, we are all called to serve God *in and through our work,* whatever our work may be.

It isn't necessary to join a monastery or become a minister to engage in work that's spiritually meaningful. There's no such thing as a vocation in the abstract—we can't say that one job is definitely a calling and another job is not. Instead, any kind of work can be a calling if—and it's a *big* if—you approach it in the right way.

The basic idea of a calling is simple yet profoundly liberating and challenging:

> *It's not what you do that's important—it's how you do it!*

Everything and Nothing

When you begin to see your work as a calling, nothing changes and everything changes. You still have your reports to write, customers to service, trucks to drive, and buildings to paint. You still encounter good days and bad days, tyrannical bosses and collegial bosses, petty-minded colleagues and pleasant colleagues. You still plead for ten minutes more sleep in the morning, and still dream occasionally of winning the lottery and retiring to Tahiti. Nothing seems to change.

But in another sense, *everything* changes. Your work is more satisfying. You don't have to struggle so hard to find meaning in what you do. As you write your reports, drive your trucks, and fix your machines, you do so with confidence that your work is imbued with meaning—all you have to do is acknowledge and embrace that meaning. You're in the right place, doing what you're supposed to do.

When this happens, you experience your life and your work as one. You no longer feel a need to compartmentalize your life and leave your personal and spiritual values at home. Your work becomes an expression of your deepest values.

In his book *Business as a Calling,* Michael Novak makes this point well. When we view our work as a calling, "it is like fulfilling something we were meant to do. It is a sense of having uncovered our personal destiny, a sense of having been able to contribute something valuable to the common public life, something that would not have been there without us—and, more than that, something that we were good at and something we enjoyed."[2]

Dealing with Frustrations

I don't want to be overly romantic about the idea of a calling. Work is still work; some days are better than others. Even if you cultivate a sense of calling, it won't make your problems disappear like magic. Work will still bring its share of stressful periods and painful failures.

But the idea of a calling can help you resist the pressure to treat your work as a curse during times of frustration and failure. It can help you to endure when things are going badly and to find ways to flourish despite adversity.

The idea of a calling puts things in perspective. It reinvigorates you by reminding you of the ways in which your work is a vehicle of love, service, and self-fulfillment. If you are ever going to find joy in your work, you'll do so by approaching it as a calling (whether or not you actually use the word).

I know this is true from my own life. Sometimes things go badly at work—I do a lousy job teaching a class, I get angry at a student, or I feel so overwhelmed by the everyday trivia of my job that I begin to doubt whether I'm in the right line of work at all. When I'm plagued by these doubts and difficulties, I cannot, by the sheer exercise of will, recapture a sense of meaning and fulfillment in my work.

But sometimes, even amidst the disappointments, I catch sight of the ways in which my job does possess elements of a calling—while meeting with a student, speaking to a neighborhood group, or sharing small talk over coffee with a colleague.

When I can link my work to my spiritual values, I find the meaning returning to my efforts. I'm not quite so tired or depressed, not quite so self-absorbed or fixated upon my own accomplishments. At these times I recognize that my students and colleagues aren't distractions to my spiritual life, but are companions along the way, from whom I receive sustenance and to whom I in turn minister.

At the same time, the idea of a calling helps me to resist turning my work into an idol. It reminds me that my self-worth isn't determined by the amount of my paycheck. There's a dimension to my work that transcends the marketplace. Service to others, creativity, self-expression—these are the most important aspects of my work. Sure, I want to do well at work—doesn't everyone? But the idea of a calling expands the notion of doing *well* to include doing *good*.

Perhaps you're thinking: This talk of calling sounds nice, but it's unrealistic and impractical. Surely it can't be that easy. Maybe some jobs are callings, but not my job. Definitely not my job!

Or you might be thinking: If a calling doesn't depend on *what I do*, but on *how I do it*, how am I supposed to do it? What attitude, what frame of mind, what preconditions are required? If I want my work to be a calling, how do I hear the call that's addressed to me?

      ★   ★   ★

As a start, it's helpful to separate two issues. The first has to do with your *choice* of work. What kind of work are you called to do? Should you stay in your present job or look elsewhere? I'll examine this issue in chapter 9.

The second issue has to do with finding elements of a calling in *whatever* work you do, even if it isn't exactly what you want or isn't completely satisfying to your soul. In that case, how can you cultivate some sense of a calling, even if it's only partial? I'll turn to this question in chapter 10.

EXERCISES AND QUESTIONS

1. Complete the following five sentences:

   I am good at...
   I am good at...
   I am good at...
   I am good at...
   I am good at...

2. Complete the following five sentences:

   I enjoy doing...
   I enjoy doing...
   I enjoy doing...
   I enjoy doing...
   I enjoy doing...

3. Compare your two lists with your current work. Does your work give you the opportunity to use your talents and skills? Does it let you do what you enjoy doing?

4. While you're working, do you ever get the sense that you're in the *right place* doing the *right thing*? How often does this happen? When it happens, where are you? What are you doing? Be specific. Does this give you any clues about your calling?

5. Ask yourself again: Where are the opportunities for creativity and self-expression in your work? For making the world a better place? Are you taking advantage of these opportunities? What more could you do?

6. Here's a tough one: What would have to happen to convince you that your present work was your calling? Take some time with this. You might want to think about it for awhile, then write down your answer. Come back to your answer occasionally and see how it changes.

HEARING THE CALL

9

What is your calling, and how do you discover it?

A calling isn't something that you create, although it requires creativity on your part. It's not something that you make, although you have to work at it.

A calling is something to be discovered, something that was there all the time but hidden, obscured, ignored. It's like a vein of gold, lying undisturbed for centuries deep underground, until a skillful and lucky miner (you!) pinpoints its location and persuades it to give up its fortune.

Remember, a calling is a summons—you have to listen for it. It's like the still, small voice of God that Elijah heard—words dancing on the wind, words that you can hear only if you quiet down and rid yourself of the noise and busyness that clutter up your life.

There are all sorts of voices calling you to do all kinds of work. Some voices tempt you with visions of wealth, status, or notoriety. Some offer power and domination. Some promise to make you feel loved and cherished. Only you can decide which of those many voices is the voice of your true calling.

What Is a Calling?

Which voice should you listen to? Michael Novak, in his book *Business As A Calling,* identifies four characteristics of a true calling:[1]

1. *A calling is unique.*

Your calling isn't mine. There's no such thing as an impersonal and generalized calling; there's only the particular summons addressed to a particular person. I'll never find my calling if I follow your dreams instead of my own. (Sadly, we often see this when a child feels compelled to join the "family business" out of loyalty rather than love.)

2. *A calling requires more than desire.*

Your calling must fit your personality and temperament.[2] It requires certain talents and abilities. Sometimes it takes years of training and education to develop the skills you need.

Often the first and hardest step in discovering your calling is to be honest with yourself about your gifts and talents. As a child I wanted to play major league baseball, but even in little league I possessed only a so-so arm and a distressing inability to hit curve balls. At the same time, I always loved words and books, reading and writing. Over many years, I discovered that the trajectory of my life—my experiences, dreams, talents, strengths, and weaknesses—pointed toward teaching and writing as the arena in which I could fulfill my personal destiny to serve and to find meaning.

3. *A calling gives a sense of energy and enjoyment.*

A calling is deeply satisfying. Not that a calling is devoid of disappointments and frustrations. No work is. But if your work is a calling, you know you're in the right place, doing the right thing, and this gives you the energy and the endurance to carry on in bad times as well as good.

Novak quotes the essayist Logan Pearsall Smith as saying, "The test of a vocation is love of the drudgery it involves." The inevitable disappointments at work are the price you must pay for the good fortune of living out your calling. It's a price you're happy to pay.

4. A calling isn't easy to discover.
Now we come to the heart of the matter: As you search for your calling, there may be years of false starts, lost opportunities, and embarrassing failures. Most of us will change jobs lots of times. Each change may be a step along the way to our calling. The virtues of patience and hope are indispensable.

The Communal Dimension

There's a good deal of common sense in what Novak says, but his analysis needs to be expanded. There are other important characteristics of a calling that deserve our attention as well.

Novak gives little weight to the *communal dimension* of the search for a calling. Introspection, self-reflection, prayer, and meditation—all these are critical for discovering your calling, but they aren't enough. Your relationships with other people are crucially important. Your calling is in large part forged in your interactions with others. Talking with friends, having lunch with colleagues, getting praise or criticism from bosses, watching family members finding their own way in the world—these are all part of the mix that goes into finding your calling.

In my own life, for example, I could never have found my calling as a teacher and writer without the support and encouragement of many people. There were my parents, favorite teachers, mentors and role models, heroes and villains I encountered in books and movies. Above all, there was my wife. When I was unhappy as a lawyer in a large firm and needed a change, she supported my search for a job as a law school teacher. When, years later, I had the dream of going to divinity school, and writing about spirituality, she cared for and tended my dream like a garden, helping to make it grow. The contours of my calling emerged during the long hours we spent talking and dreaming together.

The search for your calling is like the exploration of an unknown world. You can't make the journey without careful preparations and loyal companions. You need friends who will not only support and encourage you ("That's a great idea, why don't you try it!"), but also bring much needed objectivity and constructive criticism ("Yes, you *could* do that, but do you really think you *should*?"). Sometimes just knowing that my wife has faith in me to make the right decision and that she won't abandon me if I fail empowers me to do what I had lacked the courage or the will to do.

Deep Gladness, Deep Hunger

We also need to give more attention to the idea of a calling as an *instrument of service to the wider community*. The religious roots of the word *vocation* remind us that a calling is an invitation to use our talents to serve the community. Recall my earlier discussion of the Protestant Reformers, who taught that any work can be a calling if it's approached as a ministry to God and to neighbor.

Theologian and novelist Frederick Buechner makes this point beautifully. His words deserve to be quoted:

> The kind of work God usually calls you to do is the kind of work (a) that you need most to do and (b) that the world most needs to have done. If you really get a kick out of your work, you've presumably met requirement (a), but if your work is writing TV deodorant commercials, the chances are you've missed requirement (b). On the other hand, if your work is being a doctor in a leper colony, you have probably met requirement (b), but if most of the time you're bored and depressed by it, the chances are you have not only bypassed (a) but probably aren't helping your patients much either....The place God calls you to is the place where your deep gladness and the world's deep hunger meet.[3]

You are called to the place where your *deep gladness* meets the world's *deep hunger:* Where you can use your talents to make the world a better place, while satisfying your own needs for joy and satisfaction in your work. Meaning and fulfillment come at the point of convergence.

As Buechner indicates, a person might do "good" work but take no enjoyment from it and derive no sense of fulfillment. You might become a doctor, for example, only because it was expected of you, when your real dream was to become a musician. Your work as a doctor might be nothing but a job, or even a curse, despite its many opportunities to help others. If there's no joy in your work, you haven't found your calling.

On the other hand, you might do work that contributes nothing to the world—your work might be *de*-structive rather than *con*-structive—even though you take great joy from it. We wouldn't apply the idea of a calling to someone who took great pride in his work as a slum landlord, thief, or manufacturer of dangerous products.

But let's be careful not to judge too hastily, either. A calling is lived out amidst the particularities of a person's life and work; as I said earlier, more important than *what* you do is *how* you do it. The goal isn't to point fingers at other people but to discover for yourself the kind of work that's right for you.

I wouldn't be so sure that a writer of TV deodorant commercials, to use Buechner's example, doesn't have a calling. After all, one way to serve the world is to serve your customers by providing them with worthwhile goods and services. I would want to talk to the writer of commercials and ask her: How do you see your work? Does it provide an outlet for your skills and talents? Does it bring you joy? Do you find spiritual meaning in your work? Do you approach it as a way to make the world a better place?

The world has many deep hungers, many great needs, and there are lots of ways that our work can meet those needs. A writer of TV commercials could use her work to express her creativity and bring beauty, enthusiasm, and humor to the world—qualities that are sorely needed.

Inner and Outer Meaning

Let's summarize this idea of a calling. Recall our discussion from chapter 3. The problem with seeing your work as a job is that it has an *outer meaning* (it pays the rent) but no *inner meaning* (no meaning in and of itself). A calling has both.

With a calling, your work possesses an outer meaning—it's a way to make a living, care for your family, and so on. In a broader sense, it's a way to serve your community and leave a legacy. At the same time, your work possesses an inner meaning—it's an avenue for self-expression, an outlet for creativity, a source of joy, and a part of your spiritual life. A calling doesn't sacrifice one kind of meaning for the other.

We must be careful, however, not to conceive of a calling in too grandiose terms. A calling isn't reserved for poets, painters, and priests. If your view of a calling is too exalted, you're setting yourself up for failure and disappointment. You'll never be satisfied. You'll always be searching for something more.

To avoid this, it helps to think of a calling in more modest terms. Your calling doesn't have to be either/or, all or nothing. It can be a matter of more-or-less, something rather than nothing. As we'll see in the next chapter, you can usually find elements of your calling in your present work, even if it's not precisely what you want to do with your life. To hear your call, sometimes you have to live with the silence.

EXERCISES AND QUESTIONS

1. Look again at Michael Novak's description of the four characteristics of a calling. Do they make sense? Do they ring true in your life? Do they shed any light on your calling?

2. Which of the characteristics apply to your present work? Which are missing? What can you do to cultivate these missing elements? Be specific.

3. Look again at the first few exercises and questions from chapter 8. What are you good at? What do you enjoy?

4. Complete the following sentences:

   I experience a sense of meaning at work when...

   I am content at work when...

   I feel good about myself at work when...

   I smile at work when...

   I can see how my work helps other people when...

   I realize that my work is making a difference when...

   What do your answers tell you about yourself? About your calling?

5. Imagine that you could do any kind of work in the world—anything at all! Jot down three or four things you'd like to do (my fantasy list includes movie director, astronaut, and missionary). What

does your list tell you about yourself? About your calling?

6. Look again at the quotation from Frederick Buechner. Where does (where can) your *deep gladness* meet the world's *deep hunger*? Come back to this question often, mull it over, live with it, let it change you.

7. What do you want to leave behind as the legacy of your years as a worker? What would you like people to say about you and your work?

LIVING THE SILENCE

10

Now we come to the most difficult question of all, the make-it-or-break-it issue for any one of us who wants to approach her everyday work as a calling.

Sure, say the skeptics (and the skeptical voice inside my own head), some people are lucky enough to find their calling. But what about the rest of us who listen and listen for our calling but don't hear a thing?

What if I'm in a job that pays well but doesn't bring any personal satisfaction? Even worse, what if I'm in a job that pays poorly, offers no prospects for advancement, and provides no sense of fulfillment? What good is all this talk about calling, service, and creativity if I'm trapped in a dead-end job?

Too often we assume that the only recourse in such cases is to quit our job and try again somewhere else. As we discussed in chapter 2, some people spend their entire life flitting from job to job like bees searching for nectar, never satisfied with what they find.

Much of the popular wisdom about career planning contributes to this mind-set. Go to a local bookstore and leaf through a few books on job searches and career planning. You'll find advice about trends in the workforce and the requirements for various jobs. You'll get tips on how to network with others in your field, write an appealing resume, and make a good impression in an interview. Many of the books include questionnaires and self-tests to help you gain a better sense of where your skills, aptitudes, and interests lie.

So far, so good. But look again at these books, this time more carefully, and you'll find that many of them suffer from the same defect. They assume that finding the "right" job is completely within your control. If you try hard enough, send out enough resumes, talk to enough people, you'll find the one job that fits you perfectly.

There's another side to the coin, of course. If you don't find the right job, if you're not completely satisfied in your work, it must be your own fault. You must not be trying hard enough. You must be doing something wrong.

Some of these books do more harm than good by setting you up for frustration and disappointment. They fail to understand that a calling isn't something you do or make, it's something you hear and respond to. A calling is a summons, a summons from God, the universe, your highest and deepest self. It's not something you get by writing an attractive resume.

Moreover, for most people a calling isn't a voice heard once, clearly and unequivocally, like God speaking from a mountaintop. A calling is revealed gradually, through the twists and turns of your life's course. There are many false starts and detours. You're not in control of the process.

Some career planning books recommend that you don't take a job unless it satisfies your deepest dreams and desires. They exhort you to follow your heart and your soul—and the money will inevitably follow. But for most of us, things aren't so open-and-shut. Most of us don't have the freedom, financial or situational or psychological, to always and only do the work we love the most. Sometimes we have to take whatever we can get.

Try, Try, Try

Even if your goal is to find work that you love, how do you know what you love until you take some risks and discover what you don't love?

You may think you'd like to work with computers, think you'd like to be your own boss, think you'd like to work with people. But you don't know what talents you have and what talents you lack until you get the chance to test them. You probably won't know what gives you the greatest pleasure at work until you experience it. You might begin a certain kind of work, confident that you've embarked on your true calling, only to discover, when reality sets in, that something is missing, something is calling you along a different path.

I mentioned earlier that I worked for a time as a lawyer in a large law firm. When I took that job, I thought I had found the right work for me, but after a few years I was burnt-out and bored. I knew that I was meant to do something else, so I left to become a teacher. Looking back, I could say that I left the law firm because it wasn't my calling. I could conclude that my time there was a wrong turn, a deviation from my true path.

But that paints the experience much more negatively than it was. I gained a lot from my time as a lawyer. I was given all the responsibility I could handle. I was encouraged to be creative in my thinking. I did a lot of writing, which I had always wanted to do. I matured as a person.

Rather than interpret that time as a missed calling, or a mistake, I see it as a necessary step on the journey of my life. It wasn't the perfect job, but there were positive things about it. There were even elements of my calling in it.

A Little Bit of a Calling

This last point bears repeating—there can be elements of your calling in almost any work you do. Right here, right now, God is speaking to you. Right here, right now, there are ways to bring a little creativity, a little self-expression, and a little compassion to your work. The challenge is to find and cultivate those aspects of your work that speak to your deeper, spiritual self—even if the work as a whole leaves a lot to be desired. Often you can find a *little bit of a calling* in work that isn't everything you want it to be.

Let me give an example. I was giving a talk about spirituality and work when a woman told me that she spent eight hours a day entering data into a computer. She challenged me to explain how a job that boring, that deadening, could be a calling.

I refused to rise to the bait. Instead, I asked her a series of questions about her work and herself. I found out that she worked at a hospital, and that the data she entered into her computer was information about Medicare and Medicaid payments. If she did her job well and accurately, elderly and indigent patients got the health care they were supposed to get. If she did her work poorly, patients had to pay more money than they should or didn't get the care they needed.

I asked her why she took the job. She loved computers, she told me. And she had a large family that needed the money she earned.

"So," I said, "your work is an act of love—love for your family and love for computers. Not only that, it's a service to patients who depend upon you and the hospital for care and treatment. Is it possible to see a little bit of a calling in your work, even if it's not the perfect job for you, even if you're still searching for a job that fits your needs and gifts more closely?"

She had never thought of it that way, she conceded. She agreed (grudgingly) that her work—although it had many negatives—did contain elements of a calling that she could nurture and cultivate.

Living in an Imperfect World

My point is *not* that all jobs are created equal. My point is *not* that you should remain stuck forever in work that's out-of-sync with your desires and talents. Work that's personally satisfying and socially beneficial is a crucial ingredient of the spiritual life. Of course, you should actively commit yourself to heeding your call.

But just as important is learning to live in an imperfect world. Sometimes we end up in jobs that don't fully tap our talents or our desire to serve. When that happens, what should we do? We can complain and bemoan our fate. Or we can look again at what we're doing and focus on those aspects of work that are enriching to ourselves and others, while actively pursuing other possibilities.

E. F. Schumacher has a helpful way of looking at this in his book *Good Work.*[1] Schumacher says:

> Traditional wisdom teaches that the function of work is at heart threefold: (1) to give a person a chance to utilize and develop his faculties; (2) to enable him to overcome his inborn egocentricity by joining with other people in a common task; and (3) to bring forth the goods and services needed by all of us for a decent existence.

To the extent that your work includes these elements, it's good work. Maybe it's not great work, but it's good work! Work that isn't completely satisfying can still be good work if it lets you develop your talents, work with other people in a communal enterprise, and create helpful goods and services. If your work lets you do these things, there is a bit of your calling in it.

If, despite your good efforts, you still find it difficult to see the elements of your calling in your present work, don't despair. Part two of this book will give you some new ways of looking at your work that can help. And don't forget that work is only a part of your life; you have many other avenues to express yourself creatively, serve your community, and find joy. Take care of your family, spend time with your friends, volunteer at a school or homeless shelter, tend your garden, putter around the garage.

In other words, concentrate on the good things in your life. This will keep you from forgetting how rich your life already is. It will help you appreciate what you already have. Then, when you turn back to your work, you may be surprised to discover elements of your calling that you had overlooked—elements that you can nurture and build upon.

Think back to chapter 9 and Frederick Buechner's description of a calling as the place where your *deep gladness* meets the world's *deep hunger*. Work isn't the only place where these impulses can intersect. But your work, whatever its shortcomings, probably offers you some chance to taste that deep gladness and some chance to feed that deep hunger. That's not everything, but maybe that's enough.

EXERCISES AND QUESTIONS

1. How did you end up doing the work you do? Take a sheet of paper and draw a map or write a story that traces the history of how you got to where you are today. If you want to have some fun with this, get some crayons or markers and use different colors to show the different paths you've traveled and the various twists and turns along the way.

2. What did you learn from this history? Look especially at those pivotal moments in your life when you made a major decision or change (for me these include the decisions to quit practicing law and to attend divinity school). Do you feel that you were entirely in control of the process, or did fate, destiny, God (call it what you will) play a role? What lessons can you draw from your history?

3. To put it another way: Did you choose your work or did your work choose you?

4. I've asked this question before, but it's worth asking again and again: How does your present work fall short of your ideal of a calling? What would have to change for you to consider your work a calling? Be specific.

5. Look again at E. F. Schumacher's description of good work. Which of these qualities are being met, at least partially, in your present work? Which are missing? Is there any way to bring

some of those missing elements into your work? Don't be too quick to say *no*.

6. If your current work leaves you spiritually hungry and doesn't fit your ideal of a calling, what are you doing about it? Are you actively searching for other work, learning new skills, taking a class? If not, why not? What's stopping you?

Part Two: Cultivating the Spirit at Work

LOWERING EXPECTATIONS

11

In part one of this book, we examined the language and the images—some conscious, some unconscious—that shape our approach to work. We assessed the advantages and disadvantages of thinking about our work in various ways. And we began to explore the concept of a calling as a way to bring spiritual meaning to our work.

Now we need to take this rather general discussion and ground it in the practicalities of everyday life and work. The goal of part two is to help you (and me) transform the idea of a calling from a theoretical possibility to a lived reality.

*   *   *

In all of life, we're taught to dream big dreams and attempt great deeds. Poets tell us that our reach should exceed our grasp. Parents tell us that we can grow up to be anything we want. The media tells us that we can have it "all," that we can be forever young, healthy, wealthy, beautiful, self-assured, and loved. In sports we're told that it's OK to lose (well, maybe not OK, but it happens to everyone) as long as we give a hundred—make that a hundred and ten—percent. Anything worth doing is worth doing well.

In the spiritual life, too, we're encouraged to think big thoughts and dream lofty dreams. We're supposed to love God with our *whole* heart, our *whole* mind, and our *whole* soul. We're supposed to love everyone we meet and love them *unconditionally,* particularly our enemies. We should turn the other cheek, welcome the stranger, give our money to the poor. We should meditate, we should contemplate, we should pray unceasingly. We should focus our thoughts, discipline our appetites, control our desires. We should strive for perfection.

Saints and mystics often depict the spiritual life as a climb up a steep ladder or a towering mountain. You better be careful. One false step and you're history! In many churches, sin is understood as a missing of the mark, a failure of aim. The cure? Try harder, work longer, shoot straighter.

This is another example of the tendency I mentioned earlier for religion in the West to draw a rigid line between the secular and the sacred. Spiritual seekers are expected to break free from the snares and temptations of ordinary life. That's why the idea of a vocation was originally limited to priests, monks, and nuns—only they had committed themselves fully and unequivocally to God. Everyone else was a spiritual also-ran.

The Dangers of Thinking Big

There are advantages to thinking of the spiritual life this way. It reminds us that spirituality is important stuff, the most important stuff in life. No fooling around! No (spiritual) pain, no (spiritual) gain!

Emphasizing the *difficulty* of the spiritual life has another benefit, at least for some people. It separates the few, the proud, and the saintly from the rest of us. Only with total dedication and perseverance can you hope to become "fully alive," "whole," "self-actualized," "individualized," or "holy" (you pick the word). Those who have made the commitment and put in the work can take pride in their special status. They're part of the elect.

Where does that leave you and me (assuming you're not one of the spiritually elect, as I'm not)? The consequences for us are negative. We can never hope to equal the dedication and commitment of the spiritually enlightened. We can't help feeling doomed to failure.

That's not the worst result, though:

The real problem with making the spiritual life so difficult is that it makes it too easy!

It lets us off the hook. When the spiritual life is presented in such herculean terms, most of us can only heave a sigh—secretly, a sigh of relief—and say, "Oh, well, I could never live up to that." If you believe that you have to meditate unceasingly, deny all your humanly desires, or do great and glorious deeds like the miracle workers of old, you probably won't even make the effort. You're intimidated from even beginning. "Why bother," you tell yourself, "since anything

I could do would be so little, so trivial in comparison? Why waste the time and effort?"

The result: We end up doing so much less than we could do because we can't do it all.

But the great spiritual leaders of humanity won't let us off the hook so easily. Moses, Jesus, the Buddha, the saints and sages have all recognized that the spiritual life begins right where you are. God finds you where you're standing. The spiritual journey starts here; it starts now.

If you put the journey off until tomorrow, you'll never begin. Tomorrow never comes—each day you'll be waiting for the next, and the next, and the next. If you close your ears to the call addressed to you today, eventually you'll grow deaf to the call addressed to you each and every day.

Think Small

I talk to lots of people who crave the soulful life. They want to work and live with greater creativity, meaning, love, and compassion. They want to carve out a spirituality that satisfies the longings of their heart. Yet so often they can only think in terms of great gestures and magnificent accomplishments.

★ "I've always wanted to work with the Peace Corps," a physicist tells me, "but I don't have what they need. I need to learn a skill first."

★ "I want to open a retreat center," a doctor says, "but I need to work a few more years and save enough money to support myself."

★ "In a year or two, when my kids are older, I'm going to resign from the company and open a small consulting business to help nonprofits," says a corporate executive.

They dream such big dreams that the *perfect* becomes the enemy of the *possible*. They want to do so much that *anything less than everything is nothing*.

They could take a lesson from the American poet William Stafford. Stafford supposedly had the habit of writing a poem each day before breakfast. When he was asked how he accomplished such a feat, he replied, "Simple. Lower your expectations."

Rather than try to do too much, do *something*. The spiritual life is a life of being aware, thinking small, and living in the here-and-now. The universe is calling you right now. Are you listening?

Today at work you can nourish you soul and cultivate a sense of spirituality. It might entail something as simple as sharing a few words with a colleague who's having a problem. Maybe you should remind yourself to take pride and satisfaction in the careful and competent work you're doing—the house you're building, the report you're writing, the furnace you're fixing. Maybe you could listen to a client's story and offer a few words of advice or silent encouragement. None of these activities is necessarily soul-*less*; each could be soul-*ful* if you approach it with the right attitude.

Charles Dickens wrote of "great expectations," and there's certainly a place in life for great expectations. But there's also a place for lowering your expectations, for not biting off more than you can chew, for doing one good thing rather than fantasizing about doing many great things. By thinking small, you can actually live a bigger, richer, life. Sometimes less really is more.

EXERCISES AND QUESTIONS

1. When you hear the words *spiritual* or *spirituality,* what comes immediately to mind? Write down the first four or five things you think of. What do your answers tell you about yourself? What kind of spiritual baggage are you carrying?

2. Complete the following sentence:

   A spiritual person is someone who...

   How does a spiritual person act? Do you have to belong to a church to be spiritual? Do you have to pray a lot?

3. Are you a spiritual person? Would you like to be? Would you like others to think of you as a spiritual person, or would you consider that a fate worse than death?

4. List on a sheet of paper three or four of your spiritual heroes or mentors (they can be people you know personally or historical figures). What do they have in common? How do they differ? What makes them spiritual heroes to you? Be specific.

5. What's one thing—a little thing—you could do right now to make your work more spiritually rewarding? Why haven't you done it already? What's stopping you?

6. Consider your life outside of work. What's one small thing you could do right now to enrich your life spiritually? Will you do it? Will you do it *now*?

TEARING DOWN THE WALLS

12

One obstacle to developing a spirituality of work is the human tendency (a tendency encouraged by our society) to divide life into separate compartments or spheres. We *compartmentalize* our life, splitting it up into pigeonholes labeled "work," "family," "leisure," and "spirituality." Each inhabits its own world with its own rules.

As we discussed in chapter 4, the result is that we relegate spirituality to weekends, holidays, and a few minutes in the early morning or the late evening. Maybe we go to synagogue on Saturday or church on Sunday. Maybe we meditate for ten few minutes before breakfast, do yoga twice a week, keep a journal, or say a prayer before going to bed.

A little soulfulness in life is better than none, but this spiritual pigeonholing makes it impossible to live an *integrated* life. The most important things in life are off-limits when you're at work. Forget about your deepest dreams and desires. Forget about your needs for self-expression, creativity, service, and friendship. Forget about morals, too; morals are for the home and for the church, not for the office and the factory. At work you must be tough, efficient, amoral.

Many people live a rigidly compartmentalized life. They're good neighbors, kind to their children, respectful of the environment. They are little league coaches, ushers at church, volunteers at soup kitchens. But when they get to work, everything changes. There the dog-eat-dog mentality and the I'm-only-following-the-rules excuse hold sway. They quarantine their soul, imprisoning it in a tiny corner of life, never allowing it to exert any influence upon their work.

Most of us don't go to such extremes, but we're all tempted to live a compartmentalized life. We're all tempted to be one person at home and a different person at work. Our spiritual life suffers *whenever* we treat it as divorced from the rest of our life, as something different, something extra.

Time Won't Let Me

To get a better sense of the problem, consider a typical workday of mine. I rise early, take a shower, and dress. I get my sons ready for school and make sure they eat their breakfast. I gulp down a bowl of cereal and grab a cup of coffee. I jump in the car and drive to work. I spend my day making phone calls, preparing for classes, meeting with students, attending meetings (yuck), and squeezing in a few moments for writing. Sometimes I take an hour and go to lunch, but usually I eat a sandwich at my desk or run errands. When I get home from work, there's dinner to be made, dishes to be cleaned, the kitchen floor to be swept. Dirty clothes must be washed. The kids need help with their homework. Then there are the daily chores to fit in somewhere: shopping for food and for sneakers, picking up a prescription at the pharmacy, trying to fix a balky vacuum cleaner, paying the bills, and balancing (more-or-less) the checkbook. Often I spend an hour in the evening reading an article or a memo that I didn't get to at the office.

Finally, the kids are in bed, the house is tidied up, and I collapse onto the sofa. My wife and I spend a few minutes catching up on each other's day. I may read a book, listen to music, or watch TV, but soon my eyes grow heavy and I catch myself dozing off. It isn't long before I give up the battle and turn in for the night.

How do I fit my spiritual life into all this confusion and clutter? How do I find time for my soul? The answer is *I can't.*

There's just not enough time for the soul, not enough hours in the day. As long as I approach my spiritual life as a separate compartment, as one more responsibility, I'll always be playing catch-up, always running behind, always feeling guilty because I'm not doing as much as I know I should. *There's not enough time for the soul when the soul is one more job to do, one more chore to complete.*

What's the cure for compartmentalization? Since the problem lies in our view of life, the cure will be found there as well. We have to stop seeing our life as a bunch of unconnected parts. We have to knock down those high walls that divide our life into separate compartments. The soul, the spirit, God—this spiritual force is active in all of life, including work, home, and leisure. The religious doctrine of the incarnation expresses this fundamental truth—by becoming a human being like us, God broke down the barriers between the sacred and the profane, so that what takes place outside of church is just as important as what takes place inside.

If all of life is sacred, then we need to wake up to the holiness of the office, the factory, the kitchen table, the movie theater, and the bedroom. No place is holier than another.

A Spirituality of the Ordinary

A spirituality of work is a *spirituality of the ordinary*. It's a spirituality alert to the subtle workings of the sacred—those little moments of grace, inklings of the eternal, rumors of angels, and hints of the miraculous that are present each and everyday if we have the eyes to see and the ears to hear. God is in the details, say the theologians (so is the devil, say the theologians, but that's a topic for another day...).

An example may help. As a teacher, I spend a lot of time talking to students. Many times a student will come to my office and begin talking about a class assignment or an upcoming exam, only to open up gradually and reveal a deeper problem or concern—a family breakup, a vocational crisis, nagging doubts about self-identity. I'm embarrassed to admit that I often catch myself sneaking a peak at my watch or pretending to listen while I wonder how I'm ever going to get my "real" work done—preparation for class, writing an article—if I spend so much time with this student.

How easy it is for me to overlook the spiritual opportunities staring me in the face! At this moment, with this student, I can bring together my spirituality and my work. I can live an integrated life. But too often I find myself living in the past or worrying about the future while ignoring the present.

There's nothing mysterious or dramatic about a spirituality of the ordinary. It asks for the most ordinary of actions on our part—a kind word, an attentive ear, a smile or a laugh. When we make time and space for others, we're making time and space for our own soul, for the soul is fed by companionship and relationship.

A spirituality of the ordinary also includes a commitment to excellence. To act diligently and competently is to act spiritually. When we do good work, we're engaged in a spiritual discipline. When we do shoddy work, we're being untrue to our own creativity and to the creative energies of the universe that flow through us (a topic I'll examine in depth in chapter 16).

You can begin to cultivate a spirituality of the ordinary by reminding yourself to slow down and look around. Focus on the present. Ask yourself often: What am I doing *at this moment*? How can I live creatively and compassionately *at this moment*? How can I bring my spirituality and my work together *at this moment*?

No matter what kind of work you do, you have opportunities to develop a spirituality that honors the ordinary, the everyday, the here-and-the-now:

★ A construction worker building a house on my street asked if he could use my garden hose to cool off. As we chatted for a few moments, he told me, "I try to picture the people who'll be living in the house I'm building. It gives me a sense of pride in what I do."

⋆ A banker said to me, "I try to remember that the person sitting in front of me applying for a home loan is nervous and needs my help. The whole process of buying a house is scary; I do what I can to make it a little easier."

⋆ A friend of mine works for an airline company on a ground crew. He says, "When I service a plane, I'm making sure it's safe to fly. So I'm helping the passengers. But I think more about the people I work with. The whole crew is depending upon me to do my job. That keeps me focused on doing good work."

⋆ A colleague of mine takes her phone off the hook the moment anyone enters her office. It's her way of saying, in effect, "I'm here. I'm here with you. I'm here for you."

God is everywhere, say the mystics, or God is nowhere. The spiritual life, too, is lived everywhere, or it's lived nowhere. The soul reveals itself in everything, if it reveals itself in anything. The ordinary life is the spiritual life.

As the Gospel of John reminds us, the spirit—the same word means "wind" in Greek—blows where it wills (Jn 3:8). But the spirit cannot blow freely if we put obstacles in its path—if we divide our life into compartments and build high walls between them. The spirit blows where it wills, but only if we tear down the walls, dismantle the compartments, and get out of its way.

EXERCISES AND QUESTIONS

1. In chapter 7 I asked you to review a typical work-week. Now do the same thing with a typical work-day. Look back over your appointment calendar, if you have one. If not, write down on a sheet of paper how you spent a recent day. Make sure to write down everything connected to work—include the time you spent getting ready, driving to and from work, cleaning up afterwards, and so forth.

   Also include all the time you spent on unpaid work—making dinner, buying groceries, going to the bank, and such.

2. What did you learn about yourself and your work? How much time do you spend working for pay? Working without pay?

3. How much time do you have left for everything other than work? Subtract the hours you spend sleeping. How much time is left? How do you spend this precious time? How much of it do you spend on your spiritual life?

4. Now do the same thing with a typical weekend. How do you spend your time? How much time is spent working, either at your job (by the way, can't some of that work wait until Monday?) or around the house? How much time do you spend on your spiritual life?

5. To what extent have you compartmentalized your life? Have you built walls between work and the rest of your life?

6. If this talk of compartmentalization strikes you as vague or abstract, here's another way to get at the same issue: Are you one person at work and a different person at home? In what ways? What parts of yourself do you leave at home when you go to work? What parts of yourself do you leave at work when you go home? (If you're feeling particularly courageous, why not ask a close friend, family member, or colleague for their opinion?)

7. Think again about a typical workday. Where are the opportunities to cultivate a spirituality of the ordinary? How could you take better advantage of those opportunities? What's one thing—a small thing—you could start doing right now?

TAKING OFF
THE MASKS

13

The spiritual life requires good eyesight. We need to see things as they truly are. We need to see our work clearly: What opportunities does it offer? What risks? What challenges?

We need to see ourselves clearly: Who am I? What do I really want from my work? From my life?

And we need to see other people accurately: Who are you? How should we relate? I can't treat you as a companion on the journey of life if I think you're someone you're not.

There are lots of things that get in the way of seeing things clearly. Pride. Anger. Shyness. Greed. A bad childhood. A good childhood. Religion. Culture. Experience. But there are two factors operating in the workplace that are less obvious and therefore more dangerous to our spiritual life. These are the *masks* we wear and the *projections* we make. Let's look at each.

The Masks We Wear

We all wear a certain face at work—a *persona*, Carl Jung called it, from the Latin word for a mask worn by an actor in a play. We wear a mask (actually many masks) as we perform the many roles that make up the drama of our life. Your work persona is your usual way of adapting and appearing to the world while you're at work. It's *who you are when you are at work*. (In the same way, we could talk of the parent persona, son or daughter persona, friend or lover persona, etc.).

Jung said that "every calling or profession...has its own characteristic persona....A certain kind of behavior is forced upon them by the world, and professional people endeavor to come up to these expectations."[1] Erich Neumann put it more ominously: "The persona is the cloak and the shell, the armour and the uniform, behind and within which the individual conceals himself—from himself, often enough, as well as from the world."[2]

Say the word *lawyer*, and immediately a certain image pops into your head (keep it to yourself, please!). Say the word, *bartender* and a different image appears. Say the word *minister* and another idealized picture enters your mind. That image is like a mask or costume that the worker wears, influencing and shaping her approach to her work, often without her realizing it.

A doctor, for example, develops a certain way of dealing with her patients. Her character and personality affect her approach, but so do the expectations that surround her role. Not every doctor acts the same, but there's a common core of traits associated with the job—a common stereotype. As soon as a person puts on a white gown and drapes a stethoscope around her neck, she begins to live out this idealized image, and the rest of us begin to relate to her in certain conventional ways. We expect doctors to be competent, calm, and in charge; patients, too often, are expected to shut their mouths, open their wallets, and do what they're told.

Losing the Person in the Persona

The problem isn't that you wear a mask at work. That's probably inevitable. The problem, as George Orwell pointed out years ago, is that *the more you wear a mask the more your face will grow to fit it.*[3] Just as a Halloween mask narrows your scope of vision, your persona can distort your vision of yourself as a worker and a human being.

You begin to think of yourself not in the *first person*—as an I, a human being, a moral agent. Instead, you see yourself in the *third person*—as a thing, an it, a moral and spiritual neuter. You tell yourself that you have to act the way a banker, sales clerk, or secretary is "supposed" to act. You need to look, talk, and conduct yourself a certain way. Instead of tearing down the walls between the compartments of your life, you build even higher ones.

Jung warned of the temptation for people to "become identical with their personas—the teacher with his textbook, the tenor with his voice...." One day you wake up to find that the mask has grafted itself onto your face and can't be removed. Your person gets lost in your persona.

I've experienced this in my life. During my first years as a teacher, I felt unprepared for my role, and I tried to hide my anxieties behind a rigid mask at work. One day a student came to see me about his performance on an examination. After I explained why his grade was so low, he went off on a long rambling account of the reasons for his poor work. Finally, I cut him off and said, "Look, the grade stands." The student jerked back as if I had slapped him, picked up his paper, and ran from my office.

Later, I realized that my insensitivity was a function of my defensiveness. I was so sure that the student wanted to argue about his grade that I never heard what he was saying. All he wanted to do was explain his poor performance and let me know that he had tried his best. He wasn't looking for an argument, only a little understanding and perhaps reassurance that he wasn't bad or stupid just because he had done poorly on one exam.

How different our meeting would have been if I had listened to him in silence and then said, "Look, don't worry about it. These things happen. You had a bad day, that's all. Maybe I can give you a few tips about writing exams." But I was trying so hard to live up to my idealized (and inaccurate) notions of a teacher that I forgot to be a human being.

When your mask becomes too tight, you can lie, cheat, and hurt others—all the while telling yourself that you're not really doing it, it's not really your fault. You're just doing your job, just doing what you have to do.

Once you become aware of the risks of the persona, however, its grip upon you loosens. All you need to do is remember that you bring *all* of yourself to your work. Your hopes and dreams, insecurities and anxieties, fantasies of power and success, yearnings for self-expression and fulfillment—all of these come with you. You don't leave your moral and spiritual values at home when you go to the office or the factory.

Here's a simple way to keep your persona in check. Never ask yourself: *What would someone in my role think, say, or do?* Never: *What should a manager, secretary, clerk, or painter do?*

Always ask yourself: *What should I think, say, or do?* You play many roles in life, but your roles don't make you who you are. You're bigger than any and all of them.

Business Projections

The challenge of dealing with the persona is aggravated by the psychological impulse toward *projection*. Projection is a fancy word for a simple phenomenon. It occurs when a person refuses to acknowledge certain painful or objectionable parts of himself and throws them off (projects them) onto someone else.

Perhaps you find yourself spontaneously repelled by a new colleague at work. The new worker seems pleasant enough, yet you feel an irrational hatred welling up inside you. Nothing he does seems right; his every word or gesture seems calculated to upset or upstage you.

In a saner moment, you realize that you can't put your finger on any objective reason that would explain the depth of your hostility. Perhaps the real reason, hidden until now, is a subconscious association you've drawn between your new colleague and a high school bully who made your teenage years a nightmare or an elder brother who was always your parents' fair-haired favorite.

Sometimes the person on whom you project isn't a stand-in for another person but for another part of yourself. Let's say that you have a hard time dealing with aggression. This has made you timid and unassertive. You make no waves at work, never disagree with your boss, never get angry, never stand up for anything.

When a new worker joins your office, you take an immediate dislike to her. She's itching for a fight, you think. She's too pushy, too argumentative.

Well...maybe....But maybe she doesn't have a problem with anger and assertiveness at all. Maybe she possesses a healthy self-esteem and the courage to speak her mind. Maybe you're projecting onto her a part of yourself that you've submerged and hidden. She's living out a part of you that you've repressed. Your dislike of her says nothing about her—but quite a lot about you.

The Shadow Knows

This is what Jung called the *shadow*—those parts of ourself that we find socially or personally unacceptable and hence refuse to acknowledge. The shadow can be thought of as the reverse of the persona—the persona is the *idealized* self we present to others, the shadow is the *unacceptable* self we hide from others. Our shadow side might include feelings of anger, greed, earthiness, sexuality, aggression, and so on.

Many of us expend a lot of energy trying to sub-jugate our shadow. We go so far as to deny that we even have such distasteful passions and impulses. Me? No way! I'm not like that!

But the more we deny our shadow side, the more we project it onto others. As Anthony Storr says, "Examination of those attributes which a man most condemns in other people (greed, intolerance, disregard for others, etc.) usually shows that, unac-knowledged, he himself possesses them."[4] Jesus understood this. He told us to take the log out of our own eye rather than worry about the speck in some-body else's eye.

Let's not get too Jungian or Freudian about this. You don't have to become an amateur therapist con-tinuously psychoanalyzing yourself. Just remember that whenever you feel hostility, sexual attraction, extreme fear or anxiety, a desire to punish or to pro-tect some other person, projection *may* (*may*, not *must*) be operating. You should be alert to the possi-bility of projection whenever you have any kind of reaction that seems exaggerated or out of propor-tion—whenever you can't help thinking about a per-son, for better or worse, or whenever you find yourself putting the person on top of (or under-neath) a pedestal.

Turning Off the Projector

What's the cure for projections? They are, by their very nature, unconscious. You can't deal with them until you acknowledge their existence.

Projections are like bad dreams. They go away when the bright light of day shines on them. You can reduce their hold by looking at them honestly and observing how they operate. Treat them the same way you treat your persona—don't fight them, but watch them, and remind yourself that you're not bound by them. You're bigger than they are.

Coming to terms with your projections can motivate you to develop certain parts of your personality that have been undeveloped. Maybe it's time for you to become more self-assertive at work, rather than for a colleague to become less. Dealing with your projections can free you to accept parts of your personality that you've repressed or denied. Maybe it's you who has a problem with anger, not that colleague.

In the movie *Addicted to Love*, a man and a woman are jilted by their lovers, who take up with each other. The man and the woman find themselves spying on their former lovers and trying to sabotage the relationship. They listen in on their ex-lovers' conversations and lovemaking; they project the images of their ex-lovers upon the wall of the derelict building where they're hiding out. Gradually, the man and woman discover that their images of their former lovers are exaggerated and unreal—their ex-lovers were neither as good nor as bad as they had imagined. Then, and only then, are they free to bid goodbye to their ex-lovers and realize (in true Hollywood fashion) that they really love each other.

In the same way, when you turn off the projector in your life, you become free to relate to others as the human beings they are. You can see them with all their faults and frailties and with all their virtues and blessings. You can *choose* whom to like and not to like, whom to trust and whom to distrust, rather then being tossed about by invisible forces of which you are unaware.

Think of it this way: You're the projectionist in a movie theater. When you turn on the projector, you can't see the people in the audience. Everything but the movie is dark and shadowy. That's all well and good, if you want to watch the unreal images flickering across the movie screen. But if you want to see the real people in the theater and see them clearly and accurately, you have to turn off that projector, and turn on the lights.

EXERCISES AND QUESTIONS

1. What's the mask you wear at work? Draw a blank? If you have trouble describing your mask, could it be that your face has grown to fit it? In that case, you'll need to summon up your courage and ask a few friends from work to tell you how they see you (gulp!).

2. Complete the following sentences with the first five or six adjectives that come to mind:

   At work I am...(aggressive, confident, lazy, etc.).

   At home I am...(fun-loving, tired, boring, etc.).

   Compare your two lists. What do you notice?

3. What are one or two things you could do to loosen the mask you wear at work? A few possibilities: take things less seriously, use the word *I* when talking about yourself, bring something to your office that reminds you of what's most important in your life. What would it be like to wear no mask at all? Is that possible? Is it even desirable?

4. Think of someone you dislike at work, or someone you admire a lot. Why do you feel the way you do? Could projection be operating, at least in part? Could this other person be a stand-in for someone else or for some part of yourself?

5. What's one part of yourself that you're embarrassed or uncomfortable about accepting? You don't have to share this with anyone else—but say it out loud, to yourself. (When we name some-

thing, we reduce its power over us.) Do you ever find yourself criticizing other people for this characteristic? Could they be living out your shadow side?

6. If projection is operating in your working life, what can you do about it? Is it enough to acknowledge the fact of the projection? Or is something more called for (an apology to someone you've wronged, for example)?

Dreams of Work

14

Before I left my job as a lawyer, I had a dream that I was trapped in my office, the door wouldn't open, and I was slowly drowning in a sea of legal documents.

When my wife was trying to decide whether to quit a job that had grown intolerable, she had a dream that she was lost in a strange land. Nothing was familiar. She was about to break down and cry when an older woman appeared, laughed, and said, "Don't worry. You'll be fine." Then the woman disappeared.

Wisdom from the unconscious? Messages from God? Random electrical impulses from the brain? Whatever they are, dreams can be an important part of the spiritual life. For ages, people have turned to their dreams for wisdom and guidance. In the Bible, for example, there are many instances of people receiving messages from God in their dreams (the best-known examples are probably the two Josephs— the Joseph who interpreted the Pharaoh's dreams and the Joseph who was told in a dream to flee with Mary and Jesus from the murderous King Herod).

It's easy to become overwhelmed by the various and conflicting theories and schools of dream interpretation. But for our purposes, it's not necessary to subscribe to any particular approach. All we have to do is take our dreams seriously—but not too seriously, not literally—and let them speak to us. When we do this, our dreams can become a surprising source of wisdom about our spiritual life both in and out of the workplace.

An easy way to start is to think of your dreams as a kind of Rorschach test. Assume only that your dreams have something to say—something to say *to you, about you*. Don't prejudge your dreams or try to squeeze them into a shoe that won't fit. Just wait, listen, and watch.

Don't interpret a dream. Just stay with it. Chew on it. Let it speak to you. Let it live with you. Come back to it occasionally. Be open to the ways in which it does (or doesn't) shed light upon your life.

It helps to jot down your dreams to remember them better. Sometimes you'll experience a strong resistance to writing down a particular dream. You'll tell yourself it's not necessary to write it down, you'll never forget this dream. Whenever this happens, realize that some part of you wants to ignore the dream. Your resistance is a tip-off that the dream has something important to say to you, something you'd rather not hear. Make sure to write it down—quickly.

Dreams and Work

Once you begin to attend to your dreams, you'll find that a certain number of them (in my case, a lot) speak about your work and your relationships at work. I often dream about upcoming projects, colleagues and bosses, friends and enemies, deadlines, meet-ings, and so on. Sometimes my dreams mirror my fears—I dream about being late for an important meet-ing or going blank as I stand up to give a talk. Just as often, however, my dreams offer new ways of think-ing about and dealing with a problem I'm facing.

For example, years ago I had a dream about a colleague with whom I had a rather cool and strained relationship. We were not enemies, but no one would call us friends. We nodded politely when we met and continued on our way, but there was always an undercurrent of tension and hostility in our deal-ings. No matter what position I took in our law firm meetings, this other lawyer was always on the oppo-site side.

In my dream, my colleague invited me to his house for dinner. We were seated at his dining room table, enjoying a fine meal and good conversation. Things couldn't have been better. It seemed as if we were close friends. Suddenly, he leaned toward me, smiled wickedly, and said, "Of course, the food is poisoned."

My initial response to the dream was that it strongly corroborated my distrust of my colleague. Beware of him and his gifts. Don't trust anything he says or does.

Over time, however, I began to see things differ-ently. As I let the dream speak to me, I noticed a detail that I had overlooked. If my treacherous dining companion had really poisoned the food, then *he too would die*. He too was suffering.

Up to then, I had always assumed that I was the wronged party in our relationship. Now I saw it from the other side. My colleague as well had been "poisoned" by the fake atmosphere of conviviality we cultivated. I had to admit that sometimes I took positions on matters based not on the merits but on my dislike for him—if he was for it, I was against it. I understood that the coldness we hurled at each other returned like a ricochet to freeze our own hearts.

From then on, I tried to remember (not always successfully) that my colleague was being hurt as much as I was by our strained relations. Over time, our icy relationship began to thaw—this is no fairy tale, and I can't say that we ever became the best of friends. But we weren't so hostile toward each other. We no longer felt a righteous duty to take diametrically opposed positions. Occasionally, we even agreed on something.

I don't know and don't care whether my understanding of this dream was "correct" in terms of some scholarly theory of interpretation. I do know that it was right for me—it gave me an "ah-hah, that's it!" sensation.

You too can listen to your dreams of work. You don't need to do any complex interpretation. Just take the dream seriously, on its own terms, but not too somberly—dreams, I find, have a sense of humor. Trust that the dream will reveal itself to you in its own time and its own manner. Let your dreams be bread for your spiritual journey.

The Art of Divination

When you pay attention to your dreams, you're practicing a form of *divination*. Don't let the word scare you. Many people think of divination as an occult art practiced by "primitive" cultures—something for medicine men and shamans. But people in all times and places have practiced the art of divination. People still do. They open the Bible and read a passage at random, check their horoscope in the morning newspaper, draw Tarot cards, or consult the I-Ching.

People unfamiliar with divination often condemn it as a misguided or even demonic effort to learn what no man or woman should know—the future. Careful practitioners of the diviner's art, however, are quick to caution that their tools don't predict the future, for the future isn't set in stone and unchangeable. Divination helps us to see more clearly the forces and trends that are operating *now* in a certain direction. It's up to us how to respond to these forces.

Divination is a way of knowing that relies not on reasoning, intellect, and logic, but on intuition, feeling, and meaningful coincidence (synchronicity, as Carl Jung called it). You can use it to read the "signs of the times" for their meaning for your life. As the spiritual writer Thomas Moore says, divination is a "technology of intuition."[1] It can help you live more deeply, by helping you understand what's going on inside yourself and within your situation in life.

Divination doesn't require a visit to a fortune teller or a Tarot reader. It's not an occult or demonic art. It can be practiced anytime or anyplace by anyone. All you have to do is cultivate the same attitude of respectful attentiveness—watching and waiting—that I suggested you bring to your dreams.

Divination at Work

So, for example, you could begin to practice divination at work. When something happens that seems meaningful, coincidental, good, bad, or strange, you could ask yourself:

What's the message here for me?

What's God (the universe, my higher self) saying to me?

When you're thinking about a colleague and the colleague appears at your door; when you're working on the computer and your screen goes blank; when you misplace the key to your office or your filing cabinet; when you're writing a memo and type the word *hate* when you meant *date*; when you walk into your office building for the millionth time and notice for the first time the painting of a waterfall that hangs over the receptionist's desk—in all these cases, and many more, you can stay alert to the ways the universe is speaking to you and inviting you to listen.

I recall a time when I was feeling intense pressure because of a number of projects I was working on, each of which (according to my boss) was more urgent than the rest. One day I came to work and found that my phone line was mysteriously dead. My initial reaction was panic—now I would fall even farther behind! I immediately scooped up my files in a huge heap and started to run down the hallway in search of a vacant office with a phone that worked.

I stopped in midcourse. Maybe my broken phone was a sign to slow down and collect my thoughts. I walked back to my office, closed my door, and put my feet up on my desk. I let my mind wander, thinking of nothing in particular. A few minutes later I was idly scratching a few notes on a piece of scrap paper. As I sat there, doing nothing, I suddenly saw a way I could combine two assignments into one, cutting the work in half.

Many people are skeptical about trusting their intuition. They wonder: How can I be sure that my intuition is correct? How can I be sure that it won't lead me astray? Maybe I'll misread the signs of the times. Maybe I'll make a mistake.

Of course. There are no guarantees in the spiritual life. You might misread the signals. You might interpret them wrongly. Your own neuroses, blind spots, and projections might cloud your vision. But the same thing can happen even if you choose to ignore your intuition and rely on reason and logic alone. You still might be wrong.

Your intuition is like a muscle—if you don't exercise it, it atrophies, and so it might take time and practice before you feel confident following its promptings. In the end, divination shouldn't be viewed as an alternative to making decisions using reason, but as a complement. It gives you a bigger window on the world and your place in it.

As you begin to practice divination at work, you'll experience many of the same benefits that come from attending to your dreams. You'll get to know yourself better. You'll develop a better appreciation of when to act and when to do nothing. You'll begin to notice synchronicity all around you. And you'll find yourself more in tune with the workings of the wondrous and mysterious universe of which you are a part.

EXERCISES AND QUESTIONS

1. Make a commitment to yourself to attend to your dreams. Get a journal and keep it near your bed. Each morning, write down a few sentences about a dream you remember. Don't try to write too much; a few details will be enough to jog your memory. You can do the same thing if you wake up during the night.

   Each morning, take a few minutes to reflect upon your dream. You might free associate, using the dream as a point of departure, and let your imagination take you where it will. You might reenter the dream by sitting quietly with eyes closed and allow the dream to continue to unfold.

   You can do any of these things, or whatever else strikes your fancy. Just spend a few minutes each day with your dreams. Write down your thoughts in your journal. (Don't worry if you have trouble remembering your dreams at first; the very act of deciding to spend time with them will make them easier to remember.)

2. Attend to your dreams for a month. Go back every week or two and look at what you've written in your journal. At the end of the month, reread your entire journal. Did any of your dreams speak to you about work? Did your dreams provide you with any new ways of seeing yourself, your problems at work, etc.? Were there any dreams that you want to come back to and think about some more?

3. Make a commitment to yourself to become aware of the "signs of the times" and how they're speaking

to you, both in and out of the workplace. When something happens that's unusual, upsetting, surprising, good, bad, or odd, ask yourself:

What's the universe saying to me?

What's the lesson here for me?

What am I being asked to do (or not do)?

Take a chance. Trust your intuition. See what happens.

4. Keep track (maybe in your dream journal) of the ways in which the universe is speaking to you. Do this for a month. At the end of the month, ask yourself what you've learned about yourself, your work, and your place in the scheme of things. What does it feel like to trust your intuition? How has your life changed?

5. If these exercises prove worthwhile, why not continue to do them for another month? And then maybe another....Even if these exercises strike you as a waste of time, consider doing them for one more month anyway. Perhaps you just need a little more time to flex your intuitive muscles. Or perhaps the resistance you're feeling is a signal that something important is trying to happen.

EROS AT WORK

15

When I'm talking to a group about faith and work, I sometimes ask, "What comes to mind when I mention sexuality and work?" Invariably, after an uncomfortable silence, someone responds nervously, "Sexual harassment."

Sexual harassment is a gross parody of sexuality in which power and coercion replace love. It has no place at work or anywhere else. But love and eros should not and cannot be eliminated from the workplace. We bring our entire self to our work, and this includes our desires for intimacy. The need to love and be loved isn't restricted to the bedroom or the boudoir. Love seeks expression in our work and workplace as well.

We often overlook the erotic aspects of work because our language has no clear and precise way of talking about the erotic. In English, the word *love* is used to cover a lot of ground. It includes sexual love, a mother's love for a child, feelings of affection toward a friend, the desire for union with God. In contrast, Greek has several different words that speak to the various aspects of love—*eros* is used for sexual love, *philia* for love of friends, and *agape* for selfless love. Each of these loves can flourish at work.

For example, many people take a great, almost sensual, pleasure in their work. They love what they do. It brings them great happiness. They wouldn't (couldn't) stop working even if they inherited a million dollars and could retire tomorrow.

We aren't surprised when an actor, dancer, or musician feels this way. And we can understand why a sculptor or carpenter might love his or her work. If you're in the arts or the crafts, your work is an extension of yourself, an expression of who you are. It's natural to take delight in your work.

But we have a hard time believing this when it comes to other kinds of work. We forget that there's something beautiful and lovable in any honorable job well done. Making use of your God-given talents is *itself* a cause for celebration. As St. Thomas Aquinas put it:

> Everything gives pleasure to the extent that it is loved. It is natural for people to love their own work (thus it is observed that poets love their own poems): and the reason is that we love *to be* and *to live*, and these are made manifest in our actions.[1]

According to Aquinas, our work is an expression of who we are. To be alive is to work. To love work is actually to love life. It shouldn't surprise (or amuse) us when a banker, accountant, or mechanic loves what she's doing. Love flows from doing work you're meant to do and doing it well.

To love our work this way, we have to be convinced that it's something good, something worthwhile. Not all of us feel this way, certainly not all the time. But as we've seen throughout this book, every job offers opportunities for creativity, service, and meaning. As you cultivate these dimensions of your work, you'll begin to take pleasure in what you're doing. The little things you do at work—talking with a customer, writing a report, helping a colleague deal with a problem—will bring a bigger sense of satisfaction and even joy.

I can always tell when I'm enjoying my work. I enter a twilight zone where time has no meaning. I look at my watch and find that an hour or two has gone by. Where did it go? I was so engrossed in my work that I lost track of the time. Time does fly when you're having fun.

It's important to savor such times when they happen. How quick we are to whine when our work goes badly! We should be just as quick to take pleasure when our work goes well. We'll never love our work if we don't let ourselves appreciate it.

Friends...

There is another way in which our erotic life is lived out at work. Some of our deepest attachments and relationships are with the people we encounter at work—our colleagues, customers, clients, and bosses. I see this in my own life: Several of my closest friends work in my office. My need for the kind of love we call friendship finds expression in the workplace.

Friendships are an important part of the spiritual life. As I listen to a friend tell a painful story, as I speak in halting tones about my own failures and frustrations, as I work side by side with someone I admire and appreciate, as I relax with colleagues over lunch or coffee—as I do these things, I'm engaged in a spiritual practice. The spiritual life is lived not in isolation but in connection, in relationship.

In his book *The Re-Enchantment of Everyday Life,* Thomas Moore makes this point beautifully:

> The soul hungers for friendship just as ardently as the body hungers for nutritious food, and something as simple as friendship can make a workplace enchanting. A factory or an office can hum with the thoughts of good conversation and empathic fellowship, with fantasy about fellow workers and longing for their company. When people stand next to each other at work and have no fantasy about each other, no stories on which to dwell, and no history of interaction, then they are inanimate—not animated, not ensouled—as frigid as the machines that labor metallically around them.[2]

All the joys and agonies of friendship can be played out at work. You feel pleased and honored when a colleague remembers your birthday, seeks your advice, or sends you a congratulatory note. You feel hurt or betrayed when a colleague, whom you thought of as a friend, criticizes you in front of others, pulls rank on you, or makes a cutting remark about your appearance or your work.

Friendships don't happen spontaneously. You need to invest time and energy in cultivating them. This is a problem, because your workplace may not support this, and may even oppose it. Friendship requires talk, fantasy, the sharing of stories, laughter, and tears—none of which seem to have much to do with profitability, efficiency, and the bottom-line. Thomas Moore quotes the owner of a furniture business: "We're afraid that if we encourage friendship among employees, productivity will go down." Many bosses agree.

On the other hand, I suspect that the benefits in better morale and deeper collegiality would more than make up for any time "lost" to productivity. I know that my own attitude toward work is greatly influenced by the people around me. Nobody wants to work in a hostile environment. None of us can do our best if we work in constant fear of being criticized or yelled at for the smallest mistake. Whenever I have worked in an office where I felt respected and had good friends, I've brought passion and enthusiasm to my work. I've gone the extra mile, doing more than my job description required, rather than looking for excuses to do as little as I could.

Nevertheless, while I'm certain that it would be good business for business to support friendships among its workers, many employers are not going to see it that way. They're too afraid. Where does that leave us?

Once again, as we've seen so often, the best recourse is to think small and simple. Don't try to do too much or you'll end up doing nothing. Perhaps you can go to lunch with a colleague once a week, invite your office over to watch a sporting event or have a barbecue, make a point of celebrating with a card or cookies the birthdays of your fellow workers and their families.

Do what you can do. Sometimes deep friendships grow from friendly gestures.

...and Lovers

One of the reasons why employers discourage friendship among their employees is the fear of sexuality rearing its beautiful and ugly head. Certainly the office and the factory are fertile (a suitable word, I'd say) grounds for the blossoming of sexual relationships. Flirting is endemic. People fall in love at work all the time. Everyone knows someone who met their spouse at work. Most of us also know someone whose marriage was destroyed when one or the other spouse entered into a clandestine office romance.

Anytime people are in close proximity, as in work, sexuality is part of the mix. Put two people in the same room (or one person with imagination), and a sexual dimension is present. But there is something special about the workplace that seems to excite sexual energy. The long hours, the shared commitment to a common goal, the creative vitality, the emotional investment we make in our work—all these factors lend a passion, a sexiness, to the workplace. The masks we wear at work are calculated to hide our warts and present an image of competence and attractiveness that contributes to this erotic quality.

We've already discussed how work can be a powerful catalyst for projection. Much of this projection has a sexual component. People find themselves fantasizing about sexual escapades with their coworkers and often convince themselves that no one "understands" or "appreciates" them as much as a sympathetic and attractive colleague. They fall in love not with the real person working alongside them but with their idealized image of the person.

That doesn't mean that we should exile our fantasy life from our work. Look again at the long quotation from Thomas Moore earlier in this chapter—if we exclude our life of imagination and fantasy from the workplace, we'll turn ourselves into machines, unable to relate to our colleagues at a deep level. We'll end up compartmentalizing our lives and banishing our feelings, emotions, and values from the workplace.

Attempts at compartmentalization either self-destruct or degenerate into a kind of moral and emotional schizophrenia. We would be better off conceding that there's emotion, passion, and sexual energy at work. It's not wrong, it's natural to have a rich fantasy life about work and colleagues, even a rich life of sexual fantasy. We shouldn't feel guilty about it or wonder if there's something wrong with us or with our relationships with loved ones—we shouldn't fall into the trap of thinking "Gee, if I really loved my wife, I wouldn't have these daydreams about Donna in the next office."

If we shouldn't banish such fantasies, we shouldn't take them literally either. A sexual dream about Donna isn't a signal that you should pursue a sexual relationship with her. It's important to accept your fantasies and dreams for what they are—for what they tell you about your inner life, your longings and needs, your hungers and fears. Fantasies and dreams pursue their own logic and their own purpose. As we've seen, they tell you more about yourself than they do about the object of your fantasy. They should be taken metaphorically, not scientifically.

When we repress our fantasy life, the result isn't a sexually sanitized workplace. Just the opposite. If employers and employees took the time and effort to cultivate friendships and attachments at work, the risks of destructive office romances and sexual harassment would probably decline. As Thomas Moore says, when the erotic element is given no healthy outlet, it "floats autonomously and dangerously like a virus in search of a victim." Bottled up, it explodes, contaminating workers and the workplace.

Fortunately, there is a vaccine for this virus—it lies in recognizing and accepting a place for love and the erotic in our work and workplace. Rather than trying to banish the erotic from work, which is an effort doomed to failure, we need to find healthy outlets for its expression.

EXERCISES AND QUESTIONS

1. What did you think of this chapter? Be honest. Did you find it odd or uncomfortable to hear talk about eros, love, and sexual fantasy in a book about work?

2. How does it strike you to hear the word joy or love in the same sentence with the word work? Is "joyful work" a self-contradiction?

3. Try this. Complete the following sentences:

   I feel great joy at work when...

   I love my work when...

   Did you complete these sentences or did you draw a blank? What do your answers (or lack thereof) tell you about yourself and your approach to work?

4. Do you have any close friends at work? If not, why not? If you'd like to cultivate a friendship with a particular person at work, what's one thing you could do to jump-start the relationship? Will you do it?

5. As you begin to keep track of your dreams, notice whether you have any sexual dreams about coworkers, colleagues, bosses, etc. If so, don't be embarrassed. Don't try to interpret or decipher your dreams. Don't take them literally. Just let them be. Spend some time with them, watching, listening, waiting.

6. Have you ever been sexually attracted to someone at work? (You don't have to tell anyone else, but be honest with yourself). How long did the infatuation last? How did it end? Was there an element of projection at work? What did the experience teach you about yourself? Is there a lesson here for you?

7. Have you ever engaged in an office romance? How long did it last? How did it end? Was there an element of projection at work? What did the experience teach you about yourself? Is there a lesson here for you?

HONORING
YOUR CREATIVITY

16

When we read the Hebrew Scriptures, it's clear that Yahweh is a hard-working God.

In the book of Genesis, God creates the heavens and the earth out of the primeval chaos. When God says, "Let there be light," there's light. The heavens, the seas, and the earth; the trees, plants, and fruit; the birds, fish, and animals—God calls them all into existence with a word.

God is a potter, too. God fashions man from the dirt, breathes life into its nostrils, and transforms a moist clod of clay into a living being.

God is a kind of doctor, too. When God decides that it's not good for man to be alone, he sends a deep sleep to fall upon the man (our earliest example of surgical anesthesia), removes a rib from the sleeping man, and creates another human being, a woman, out of the rib.

These stories teach us something profound about work and creativity. Creative work is what God is about. God can't help but create. There's something sacred, holy, godlike, about creative work.

These stories teach us something important about human beings, too. According to the Bible, we are made in God's image and likeness. We too are made for creative work; it's part of who we are. Pope John Paul II has spoken often and eloquently of work as a sharing in the creative activity of God; in a sense, human beings are cocreators with God. Theologian Mary Daly goes so far as to say, "It is the creative potential itself in human beings that is the image of God."[1]

In short, *we are created to create*. Our work is one way to express this creativity. As Willis Harmon and John Hormann say, *"Fundamentally, we work to create, and only incidentally do we work to eat."*[2]

Creativity and Work

All creative activity is a form of work. Recall my earlier point that all work, whether paid or unpaid, requires effort. Work is hard work, and creative work is no exception. Only the person who has never tried to create could imagine that the creative enterprise comes easily or effortlessly.

Work, of course, isn't the only outlet for our creativity. Some people belittle the creativity that is done out of sheer love and joy rather than out of the need to earn a paycheck. As if the creativity in planting and tending a garden, or carving a wooden model, or knitting a sweater is inferior to the creativity of planning a corporate takeover or preparing a marketing strategy.

They're wrong. The creative impulse takes an infinite variety of forms, and none of us are in the position to judge one creative act as necessarily higher or better than another (which doesn't stop the critics from telling us what we "should" like or dislike). But this much is certainly true: You need to find ways to express your creativity. If you don't find a way to honor your creativity, you'll pay the price for being less than the person you were meant to be.

If you're not true to your deepest creative self, you'll probably become depressed and dissatisfied with life. You may feel as if nothing you do really matters or is worth the effort. A dark cloud of meaninglessness may descend upon you. Perhaps you'll try to escape this nagging sense of futility through alcohol, drugs, or mindless entertainment. Perhaps you'll grow cynical and critical of others—or (worse yet) you may come to hate yourself for wasting your time and talents. At your deathbed you may discover that while you lived for many years you were never truly alive.

Getting Out of the Way

If you want to find meaning, purpose, and joy in your work, you need to cultivate opportunities for creative self-expression. These opportunities exist for everyone, although it's easy to overlook or ignore them. Too often we assume that only the artistic genius—the novelist, the dancer, the musician—is truly creative. That's just another example of something we've seen time and again: How easy it is to think that life demands from us something big and bold, the dramatic gesture, the extraordinary accomplishment.

Here, as elsewhere, the antidote to such self-defeating grandiosity is to think small, keep your feet on the ground, and lower your expectations.

Wherever you are, whatever you're doing, that's the raw material from which you can create. God, after all, used a clod of dirt! M. C. Richards reminds us, "The creative spirit creates with whatever materials are present. With food, with children, with building blocks, with speech, with thoughts, with pigment, with an umbrella, or a wineglass, or a torch."[3] Or with a computer, a dump truck, a public relations brochure, a memo, or words spoken to a client or colleague.

Richards has a helpful suggestion about how to tap into our creative wellsprings: "We have to trust the invisible gauges we carry within us. We have to realize that a creative being lives within ourselves, whether we like it or not, and that we must get out of its way, for it will give us no peace until we do."

Her advice provides a good rule of thumb:

Trust the creativity within you—and then get out of its way!

I can attest to the wisdom of this advice in my life and the lives of my friends. I think, for example, of a friend of mine who always loved painting and dreamt of going to art school. Life had other plans for her, however, and she ended up a successful business-woman running her own insurance agency. What could be more removed from the world of the artist?

My friend still paints a little as a hobby, and that is one vehicle for her creativity. But her primary means for expressing herself is through her work. When I asked her if her work satisfied her creative longings, she told me, "What I love about art is the way you start with just the barest hint of an idea. Then, little by little, it takes shape as you let yourself go and see what happens. I try to bring that same sense of wonder and acceptance to my work. Each time I meet a new client it's a new opportunity. I never know what lies around the corner. All I know is that the client has a need. Maybe, if we sit and talk, we can figure out a way to meet that need."

My friend does what Richards recommends. She trusts the creativity within her, and then she gets out of the way. She's found a way to express her love of art in her work, not in the same way it would be expressed in painting, but in a way that's creatively satisfying nonetheless.

My friend reminds me of someone I met recently who is a fine chess player and lover of crossword puzzles. After trying a number of different jobs, he decided to become a high school teacher. He teaches foreign languages. Why this work? "Because," he told me, "learning a language is a lot like doing a puzzle." He took his love for games and found a way to express it in his work as a teacher.

That's what it means to trust your creativity and get out of the way. It means having faith that the creativity buried deep within you will find its own way of reaching the surface. It means getting rid of preconceptions and expectations—no more *I should be doing this* or *I should be accomplishing that.* The creative spirit answers to its own laws, not yours, and you can't insist that it take precisely the form you would prefer.

I know from personal experience how frustrating and self-defeating it is to fight against your own creativity. All my life I've wanted to write, but for many years I thought of myself as a novelist in waiting. I wanted to write the great American novel and find myself sitting atop the best-sellers' charts. But when it came to actually writing, that was another story. I left half-written stories in my wake wherever I went. I scribbled ideas on ragged pieces of paper and stuffed them into my pockets. I began countless journals and diaries only to find my willpower and pen power petering out after a few days.

One day I sat down and wrote a five-page essay about the spiritual life. I wrote it in a few hours, sent it to a magazine on a lark, and was happily surprised when the article was immediately accepted and published. My first small success emboldened me to try more. Eventually, I discovered that I had a certain gift for writing about spirituality and everyday life.

I still dream occasionally of writing that bestselling novel, but as soon as I turn to fiction, my creative reservoir dries up. When I return to my personal essays, however, my creative juices return and I find myself excited and invigorated by my writing. I never run out of things to say.

It's a question of being honest with myself about my calling and my creativity. I've learned to respect my gifts, and respect my limitations as well. My creative dream has been satisfied—but not in the way I had imagined.

Fueling the Fires

Many people find it hard to honor their creativity. They believe that everyone is capable of doing creative work—everyone else, that is. They take an almost perverse pride in berating themselves for how barren and lifeless their own work is.

After I gave a talk on faith and work at a local church, I was accosted by a middle-aged banker who told me that he spent his days processing home mortgage loans. He insisted that his work gave him no outlet for his creativity. When I asked him what he would rather be doing, he was silent.

"Is there any way you could approach your work differently to express some of your creative energy?"

"No," he said with a huff.

"Is there anything you do, any part of what you do, that makes you feel good or gives you a feeling of satisfaction?" I asked.

"Nothing."

"Are you good at what you do? Do you do good work?"

"Yes," he admitted, "but I hate it. I don't take any pride in it."

"Maybe that's the problem," I suggested. "Maybe you could start by taking some well-deserved pride in your work. Doing good work of any kind is an expression of your creativity. You're doing something and you're doing it well. You're making something. You're creating something."

Perhaps this man believed that he wasn't being sufficiently creative because he hadn't discovered the perfect outlet for his creativity. Perhaps he dreamt of being a poet or an artist. Or maybe it was easier to complain about his lack of creativity than to claim his creative potential. Maybe it was easier to do nothing than do something.

My suggestion was that he reverse his way of

thinking: Find something in his work that was a source of pride, something he could feel good about. Then nurture and build upon that aspect of his work. By doing so, he would fuel the fires of his creativity and provide a basis for further growth.

I would give the same advice to you, or to me: Find one thing in your work that you're proud of, one thing that's creatively satisfying, and see if you can build upon that. Once you admit to yourself that you're a creative person, doing creative work, you affirm your creative self-identity—and once you do that, you'll begin to see more and more ways to express your creativity. By acknowledging your creativity, you put yourself in touch with the fundamental creative energy at the heart of the universe. As Shakti Gawain says, "The universe will reward you for taking risks on its behalf."

Once again, you need to be realistic. No work is perfect. No work is satisfying all the time. But when you find an outlet for your creativity, you will also find it easier to put up with the drudgery that any work entails. The boredom and the difficulties are the price you have to pay to enjoy the benefits of creatively satisfying work.

I don't mean to imply that people who are trapped in dull, dead-end jobs shouldn't actively pursue another job or outlet for their creativity. In fact, a good test to determine if you're in the right kind of work is to ask if what you're doing offers sufficient opportunities for self-expression and creativity. The lack of creativity in your current work could be a signal that it's time for a change.

But as we discussed earlier, for many of us the real challenge is to stay where we are and find ways to deepen the creativity in what we're already doing. Like the God of Genesis, we are creators at our core. And like the God of Genesis, we can create new and beautiful worlds if we allow ourselves to speak the creative word within us.

EXERCISES AND QUESTIONS

1. Review a typical workday. Where are the outlets for your creativity? If at first you draw a blank, look again. This time focus on the little things you do, the ordinary things, not the dramatic. See anything?

2. What's the single *most creative* part of your work? The most exciting, the most satisfying thing you do? How often do you get to do it? How do you feel when you do it? Can you think of a way to tap into this creative energy and extend it to the rest of your work? Be specific.

3. What's the *least creative* part of your work? The most boring, most deadly, most God-forsaken thing you do? How often do you have to do it? How do you feel when you do it? Does it have a deadening and depressing effect on the rest of your work? Be specific.

4. Review the quotations from M. C. Richards in this chapter. Do they make sense to you? Have you ever had the experience of trusting your creativity and getting out of its way?

   If you're drawing a blank, try to think of a specific incident at work in which you brought your creativity to bear on a problem or project. What did it feel like to trust your creativity? How did it turn out? What did you learn about yourself? Can you think of anything happening at work right now that you might handle in the same trusting way?

5. How do you express your creativity outside of your work? What activities provide an outlet for your creativity? Is there a way you could tap into that same creative energy when you're at work? Be specific.

6. Is there a creative activity you've always wanted to try but haven't? For example, maybe you've wanted to plant a garden, play the guitar, or learn a foreign language. What's holding you back? What's keeping you from starting right now?

7. There are lots of resources for people who are interested in developing their creativity. My favorite is Julia Cameron, *The Artist's Way: A Spiritual Path to Higher Creativity* (New York: Tarcher/Putnam, 1992). It's a great book with great exercises. Take a look at it.

LOVE MADE VISIBLE

17

There's a lot of talk these days about so-called New Age spirituality. Critics complain that it puts so much emphasis on the individual quest for self-actualization that it ignores the social dimensions of the spiritual life. True spirituality, they insist, is more than a matter of prayer, contemplation, and meditation—it's equally a matter of love, service, and compassion.

These critics are probably overstating the individualistic tendencies of New Age spirituality (which, of course, isn't one spirituality but many, just as there isn't a single Christian spirituality or a single Buddhist spirituality). But they're certainly right to focus on the importance of love and service in the spiritual life.

The world's religious traditions understand this. Judaism teaches us to love our God and our neighbor as ourself. Buddhism counsels us to have compassion for all sentient beings. Islam preaches the importance of charity to the poor and needy. And Christianity exhorts us to love one another as God has loved us.

Human beings aren't solitary atoms whirling about in space—no man, no woman, is an island—but communal beings. Our identity is forged in our encounters and relationships with other people. As the philosopher Martin Buber says, "In the beginning is the relation."[1]

We are created to live with and for others. One of the great paradoxes of the spiritual life is that we find our true self by losing it—we become who we're meant to be when we spend less time thinking about ourselves and more time thinking about others.

Work as Service

If service to others is an essential part of the spiritual life, then it's an essential part of a spirituality of work. The very idea of a calling, as we discussed earlier, is tied up with this notion of service. Recall Frederick Buechner's words from chapter 9: "The place God calls you to is the place where your deep gladness and the world's deep hunger meet."[2]

A calling presupposes a willingness to feed the world's many deep hungers. Even a hermit, living alone in the desert, understands that he's a member of the human family—and so he lifts up his life and his prayers on behalf of the human community of which he's a part.

There are many ways to cultivate this dimension in our work. Some of us have a head start because we work in the so-called "helping" professions—medicine or nursing, for example. In that case, the link between work and service is direct and clear. Or we might work as a teacher, counselor, or firefighter. These are all occupations that exist in order to serve the community.

Maybe you can't see such a direct link between your work and serving others. In these cases, it often helps to step back from what you do each day and look instead at the larger mission of your institution or employer.

A woman who's a computer programmer at a large university told me that she often doubts whether she's helping other people by her work. After all, she spends most of her time handling payroll records of employees.

As we talked, however, I encouraged her to look at the bigger picture. Her employer was founded to educate students. It prides itself on its commitment to moral values and ministry to the underprivileged. This woman's work may not seem like service—it certainly isn't as dramatic as an emergency room physician or a crisis counselor—but she's helping the university function and function well. Her employer cannot meet its mission to its students, staff, and community without the day-by-day work of employees like her.

Or consider a person who works in a manufacturing plant making consumer goods, or in a warehouse where the goods are stored, or in a retail store where the goods are sold. At first glance, these workers may not seem to be engaged in service, but look again. These workers are manufacturing and distributing goods to customers—goods that help, in some small way, to improve the lives of the people who purchase them. Isn't this a kind of service?

Once again, it helps to think small and lower your expectations. It's easy to overlook the opportunities for service in your work if you keep your eyes focused upon the great and the grand. You don't have to find a cure for AIDS or put an end to world hunger, but you have to do *something,* something to help your community and your world.

A Ministry of Presence

Another area of work that offers opportunities for service lies in our relationships with colleagues, customers, and other people we encounter at work.

I like to call this type of service a *ministry of presence.* Years ago, I served as a summer chaplain on the Alzheimer's unit at a large hospital. All summer my advisor challenged me to put into words what I was trying to accomplish as I worked with thirty severely demented old women. Most of what I had learned about good pastoral care seemed irrelevant. I couldn't engage in serious conversation with most of the patients; certainly I couldn't hope to counsel them in any of the customary ways I had been taught. Even during Sunday services I never knew for certain how much of what I was saying actually pierced the thick fog of disorientation that permanently encircled the women.

Finally, near the end of the summer, as my advisor again pressed me to articulate my vision of ministry, I blurted out, "It's a ministry of presence, a ministry of just being there!"

Many years passed before I realized that I was called to a ministry of presence not only while serving as a chaplain, but throughout each and every day of my life. For me as a teacher, the invitation to serve others is as close as the student who sits across the desk from me and shares her story.

You too have ways to cultivate a ministry of presence in your work. No matter what you do, or where you do it, you interact with other people, and while you cannot control how they will relate to you, you can decide how to relate to them.

A clerk at a large supermarket told me that she tries to bring a friendly attitude toward her work. "It may not be much," she said, "but even in the few seconds I have with my customers, they can tell the difference between a clerk who's grouchy and a clerk who's friendly. It's not much, but I do what I can do to brighten up the day for my customers. And by doing that, I make the day better for myself, too."

Maybe you can stop by the desk of someone whose father died recently and ask how things are going. Perhaps you can invite a new colleague, who just moved halfway across the country, to have dinner with a few of your friends. Or send an e-mail to a client who just got a promotion congratulating her on her success. Sometimes all that's needed is a smile, a laugh, or a willingness to listen attentively to another person and treat her with respect.

This approach to work can have surprising consequences. When dealing with difficult customers, grumpy colleagues, or dictatorial bosses, it's easy to reciprocate in kind. How dare he do that! I'll show him! But if you approach the relationship as an opportunity for ministry, it's possible that your conduct will set the tone for the relationship. Your decency and good will might defuse a tense situation. It might lead the other party to respond in kind. Even if it doesn't, you are better off, and your spiritual life is better off, when you approach each relationship as an invitation to engage in a ministry of presence.

Transforming the Workplace

Sometimes you discover opportunities for service in unlikely places or situations. A friend of mine attended an important meeting called by the CEO of his company to decide whether to move a manufacturing plant from the United States to Latin America. My friend listened as the accountants and the lawyers gave their opinions. He heard about the money that could be saved by the move.

Finally, summoning up his courage, he spoke in a halting tone, "But what about the employees?" All eyes turned on him.

"I've already explained that we have the legal right to move," snapped one of the lawyers.

"Yes, I know," said my friend, still quietly, "I know we can do it—but what about the employees?"

The CEO looked up from his piles of paper. "Yes, what about the employees?" he asked. My friend's few words sparked a long and passionate discussion about the impact of the move on the employees. In the end, the company did relocate, but offered its workers the option of taking a position at its other U.S. plants or receiving a generous severance package.

By speaking up, my friend was living out his vision of work as a form of ministry. He reminded the company bosses that there were real people—people with homes and kids and bills to pay—who would be affected by the decision. To bring a word of compassion, of love, to the corporate context might seem courageous to some, and foolhardy to others. Whatever it is, it's definitely a form of service to the company and, beyond that, to the community.

My friend's example reminds us that the call to service starts with the people we meet each day, but doesn't end there. We live in an interconnected world, and each of us must do what we can to create a more just, humane, and compassionate workplace.

If the pressures of the workplace make it difficult to do good work and rob us of time for ourselves and our loved ones, the solution isn't just to slow down and catch our collective breath (although that would help), but to reform the workplace. If our company puts so much emphasis on the bottom line that the human soul is forgotten, then the solution isn't just to cultivate our own spiritual lives (although that would help), but to challenge the company to rethink its mission and its method. As one writer puts it, "[S]pirituality is about seeking and responding to God's presence. Good policies and humane institutions make it easier to see God. Therefore, far from being a distraction, the reform of institutions is a key ingredient to a spirituality of work."[3]

Here, too, it's tempting to think so big that you feel helpless to do anything at all. You don't have to march into your CEO's office, mobilize the workers to fight company policies, or testify before a grand jury. Look for small opportunities to transform your workplace into a more humane and loving institution. Model the kind of behavior you'd like to see—if you want justice, treat others justly; if you want compassion, practice compassion. If you want to transform the world, the transformation has to start with you. But like ripples in a pond, your life radiates outward—as you change yourself, you are changing your world.

Family Services

If you're still having trouble seeing your work as a form of service, consider the people who depend upon you for support. I think of some of my relatives who had to work two jobs all their lives to provide for their families. These men and women didn't search for "meaning" in their work. They didn't seek "self-expression" or "fulfillment."

They worked because they had to. There was nothing romantic about their commitment to hard work. They would have scratched their heads in bewilderment if told that their work possessed a spiritual meaning. (They certainly wouldn't have been caught dead reading a book like this!)

Despite their unromantic and even cynical approach to work, however, there was no doubt about one thing: They worked to take care of their families. They worked to put bread on the table and clothes on their children's backs. Family came first.

Here is another way that your work can serve as an instrument of service. Many people feel stuck in dead-end jobs, but they endure the monotony in order to provide for their families. Many spend long hours at backbreaking labor, but tough it out because their loved ones are depending upon them. Many have had to put their own dreams on the back burner to earn a living for their family.

Looked at in this way, your work is a ministry to those you love and care for, regardless of the details of what you do. The mere fact that you get up day after day, go to the office or the factory, and put in a full day's work for a full day's pay, is your way of honoring and serving those you love.

The poet and mystic Kahlil Gibran put this beautifully when he said, "Work is love made visible."[4] It's easy to say "I love you." Words are cheap. But love is only a word, only a dream, unless and until you make it concrete in your actions.

Work embodies and expresses your love. Work makes it visible. Work makes it real.

EXERCISES AND QUESTIONS

1. Look again at your responses to the exercises and questions that accompany chapter 9. Ask yourself again: How does your work feed the world's deep hungers?

2. Consider Kahlil Gibran's quote, "Work is love made visible." What does this mean to you? How does it relate to your life and work? Be specific.

3. Does Gibran's quote strike you as too touchy-feely? Too abstract and idealistic? If so, make it more concrete:

   Take a sheet of paper and list all the ways in which your work helps other people. All of them! Don't forget all the ways you help your employer fulfill its mission. Don't forget all the ways you help colleagues, customers, and so forth. Don't forget all the ways you help family, friends, and others who depend upon you for support.

4. How do you (can you) help to make your workplace more just, loving, and compassionate? What needs to change, and how can you help to change it?

5. If you're still having trouble seeing your work as a form of service, maybe you're being too modest. Ask yourself this: How would your place of work change for the worse if you were gone? ("There'd be nobody else around to make dumb jokes," a friend told me. That counts, I assured her.)

6. Do you practice a ministry of presence in your work? Don't be too quick to say *no*. Many people do this without even realizing it or making a big deal about it. If you are engaged in a ministry of presence, how can you expand your ministry? What's the next step? Are you willing to take that step?

7. If you're not practicing a ministry of presence right now, could you begin to do so? What would have to change? Are you willing to make the change? What's holding you back?

PRACTICING WHAT YOU PREACH

18

There's a whole academic discipline—chock full of books, articles, and college courses—that focuses on the relationship between work and ethics (or morality; I'll use the words interchangeably). It's usually called "business ethics." But business ethics concentrates so much on companies and their responsibilities that it usually ignores the people who make up the companies. Business ethics gives precious little guidance to the worker—not the company president, not the CEO, but the average worker—who's facing an ethical problem at work.

Most of us face ethical issues at work that are less dramatic but just as challenging as the issues dealt with in a business ethics course. Most of us won't have to decide whether to market in a third-world country a product that's legal there but illegal in the United States. But we will have to decide whether to lie or tell the truth, treat our colleagues with respect or disrespect, act fairly or unfairly, summon up the courage to speak or keep our mouth shut in cowardice. These are the kinds of issues that business ethics usually ignores.

The other problem with business ethics is that it's too philosophical. It focuses too much on learning how to reason your way to the "correct" result in a particular case. Ethics is reduced to an analytical skill, a kind of mathematical puzzle or mind game.

But ethics is more than a matter of reasoning to a result or learning how to apply philosophical principles (most of which have Greek names that even philosophers can't spell). Ethics has to do with character—with virtue, to use the quaint old word—as much as it has to do with philosophical principles. Ethics isn't really about cases or problems. It's about you.

Spirituality and Ethics

A better approach is to recognize that your spiritual life can't be divorced from your moral life. Your *spirituality implies a certain morality.* In fact, spirituality—in the broad sense we've been considering it—is the very foundation of ethics. Spiritual questions come before ethical questions.

First you have to decide: *Who am I? Who do I want to be? How do I see myself and my life?*

Only then can you hope to answer the questions: *What should I do in this particular case? How should I resolve this problem?*

Here's an example. Let's say that you're faced with the question of whether or not to accept a bribe. You could apply philosophical principles and try to determine when, if ever, it's justifiable to take a bribe. You could slowly and methodically reason your way to an answer.

I doubt if that's what you'd do, however. I doubt if you'd engage in that sort of calculation. Rather than reasoning about whether to take the bribe, you'd either accept it or reject it. You'd pocket the money or turn it down and walk away.

Why? The answer is that your character—your spirituality, really—provides the context in which such issues are encountered. Your decision whether to take a bribe depends upon your understanding of who you are and who you want to be. The kind of person you are makes certain moral choices *inevitable* and others *unthinkable*. There are two sides (at least) to most ethical issues; they rarely have a simple and unequivocal "right" answer that everyone accepts. But that doesn't mean there are no answers. There are answers that are right for you, given your vision of the meaning and purpose of your life.

The importance of character is especially clear to anyone who has ever tried to teach a child the difference between right and wrong. We tell our children to obey the laws of society, of course, but we don't teach them complex formulas for reasoning about moral issues. We don't force them to memorize philosophical principles. Instead, we teach them through our example (much to our distress, at times). We provide them with models, stories, maxims, and traditions that seek to inculcate in them a certain kind of character.

Ethics at Work

This link between spirituality and ethics means that ethics in the workplace is largely a matter of the habits and attitudes you bring to your work rather than your skill at reasoning to conclusions. It's more a matter of how you handle the little, everyday things rather than the big crises.

This is an important point, a point we've seen before:

> *If we take care of the little things, the big things take care of themselves!*

If you respect other people, if you're kind, if you're fair, if you tell the truth—if you do these things each and every day, you'll develop the inner reserves of character that you'll need when a major problem or crisis arises.

When you fill out those pesky reimbursement forms after taking a business trip, do you pad the bills a little, because "everyone does"? When you fall behind on a project, do you look for someone else to blame? When you're preparing a memo or painting a house, do you cut corners because nobody will find out anyway? When you feel snubbed or slighted by your boss, do you take it out on your subordinates?

The little things are the important things. We become the person we are by the slow, almost imperceptible accretion of little choices, little decisions. Thomas Morris puts it well:

> Whenever you make a decision, whenever you act, you are never just doing, you are always *becoming*....Every little decision is like plunking

a pebble into a pond. It never just sinks to the bottom. It always sets up ripples. Every action we perform leads to a slight tendency to do a similar thing again, sets up a pattern, begins to establish a habit....We are talking about every piece of other-regarding behavior, every piece of work that crosses the desk, every person who comes in the door. How do we treat this situation? How do we treat this person? Unless we begin moving in the right direction with respect to all the little things, we will never be in a position to make the right decisions with the big things.[1]

This way of thinking provides a kind of compass, or road map, for your moral life at work. It won't resolve all the difficult issues, of course, but no principle or formula can do that. At least this way of looking at ethics puts the emphasis where it belongs—on the everyday choices you make and the person you're becoming.

Rules of the Road

If you think of the moral life as a journey and your character as a road map, then it helps to have a few rules of the road to make your travel go smoothly. These rules of the road aren't mathematical formulas to help you reason through ethical problems. They're more like the accumulated wisdom of the ages crystallized into a few words. They may seem trite, almost cliché, but that doesn't make them any the less true:

★ Act toward others the way you'd like them to act toward you.

★ The Golden Rule is still golden today.

★ Try to see the world through other people's eyes. As Atticus Finch says in the memorable book, *To Kill a Mockingbird*, "You never really understand a person until you consider things from his point of view...until you climb into his skin and walk around in it."[2]

★ Put first things first. Figure out what's most important and keep your focus on it when you feel yourself overwhelmed by trivia. Ask yourself: What really matters here?

★ Decide what's for Caesar and what's for God. What's worth compromising about and what's worth drawing a line in the sand about.

★ Put people first. People are more important than things. Relationships are more important than accomplishments.

★ It's nice to be right, but when in doubt, opt for kindness over rightness.

★ It's important to be fair, but when in doubt, opt for love over fairness.

★ Take responsibility for your actions. If you've made a mistake, admit it. If you've done something wrong, don't search for excuses, justifications, or scapegoats. Admit your mistake, resolve to do better, and move on.

★ Ask yourself what you want written on your tombstone. Do you want to be remembered only for your work? Do you want to be remembered as a successful business executive who made lots of money and drove a fancy imported car? Or as someone who loved the world and tried to make it better?

And perhaps the most important rule, the one that encompasses all the rest:

> *Practice what you want to become, because you'll become what you practice the most.*[3]

Who you are determines what you do—and what you do each and every day determines who you become. Practice what you preach, because practice does make perfect.

It's clear from these rules of the road that ethics cannot be divorced from character and spirituality. Business ethicists are wrong if they try to treat ethics solely as a matter of reasoning and logic. In fact, work is the place where your ethics and your spirituality converge. Your spirituality molds and shapes your ethics—and your ethics reflects and reveals your spirituality.

EXERCISES AND QUESTIONS

1. Take this brief ethics inventory. Answer the following questions on a sheet of paper. Take your time answering:

   Who or what have been the three most important influences on your understanding of right and wrong? Why these three?

   Who are three of your moral heroes (alive or dead)? Why these three?

   What three things do you value the most in life? Why these three?

2. Now for the hard stuff. Answer the following questions on a sheet of paper. Take your time.

   Who are you?

   Who do you want to be?

   What do you want to be remembered for?

3. Make sure to write down your answers to these questions. Make a promise to yourself to go back and look at your answers in a month. See if your answers have changed.

4. Think back to an ethical issue or problem that you faced at home recently. What was the problem? How did you handle it? Do you feel good about the way you handled it? Do you wish you had done anything differently? Is there a lesson here for you?

5. Now think back to an ethical issue or problem that you faced at work recently. What was the problem? How did you handle it? Do you feel good about the way you handled it? Do you wish you had done anything differently? Is there a lesson here for you?

6. What ethical temptations do you face at work? It might be something as small as stealing a few pens from the supply room or something as big as falsifying a report in a million-dollar transaction. How have you dealt with these temptations in the past? Are you satisfied with how you've handled them, or would you like to handle them differently in the future?

7. What is there about your work that makes it hard to do the right thing (a demanding boss, a big expense account, your financial needs, etc.)? Be specific. What can (what will) you do to resist these pressures?

8. It's tough to deal with ethical issues all by yourself—is there someone at work or at home you can talk to about these things? Do you?

BALANCING THE WORK OF A LIFE

19

I have a couple of friends who do a good job of leaving their work at work. They keep it in proper perspective—they enjoy their weekends and evenings, spend time with their kids, take walks, and watch TV, with scarcely a thought about the report left undone at the office, the big meeting tomorrow, the project due next week.

I'm not so lucky, and you're probably not either. If I hear one refrain from working people, it's their almost desperate desire to achieve the right balance between their work and the other areas of their lives. Too often work insinuates itself into all their waking (and, sometimes, their sleeping) hours.

There are lots of reasons for this, some of which we've already mentioned. For most of us, work is an important part of our self-identity. What we do and how we do it makes a difference. (If it didn't, we'd be treating our work as a curse.) It's all too easy, however, to give our work too much importance, or even to turn it into an idol.

The pressures of the modern workplace accentuate these tendencies. We live in the age of instant communication—voice mail, e-mail, and faxes—which often translate into instant obligations. We feel constantly under the gun, out of time, out of breath, and behind schedule. Whatever's due was due yesterday!

Corporate downsizing, government reorganization, technological advance and technological obsolescence, the globalization of markets, the corporate cult of the short-term and the bottom line, the rising tide of job insecurity—these and other trends increase job stress and anxiety and make it more difficult to view our work realistically and keep it within manageable limits.

Home Work

Consider another recent development. More and more people now work at home. A friend of mine runs a computer repair service out of his house. Another friend makes pottery in her basement. Another is an investment counselor, using her laptop as her movable office.

For people with small kids, people suffering from disabilities or health problems that impede mobility, people who want more freedom than the traditional nine-to-five job offers—for many of us, the opportunity to work at home is one of the greatest benefits of our high-tech culture.

But there can be severe drawbacks to working at home. The biggest challenge is the near-impossibility of keeping your work from taking over the rest of your life. People who work at home wake up in the middle of the night to work on a project, steal a few minutes on the phone or the computer when the baby falls asleep, use their bedroom dressers (and often their beds) as filing cabinets and work space, bring cell phones to little league games and orthodontists' offices so as not to be "out of touch," and so on. It's impossible to keep work in its proper place when it's all over the place!

Those of us who don't use home as our primary workplace can sympathize with these problems. The extra bedroom in my house is often filled with exams I'm grading. Many evenings I slip away for an hour or two to read an article or prepare a talk. Occasionally, I work at home for a day—and can't resist calling my office three or four times to check my voice mail for messages.

What it all boils down to is that the line between home and work has grown increasingly blurry. It isn't clear anymore what constitutes work space and what constitutes private space. We're no longer certain what time is for work and what time is for family, friends, and leisure. It's easy for work to become a glutton that devours the entire week and leaves not a crumb for the rest of our life.

How can we cultivate a sense of the sacredness of work and life under such pressures? How can we hope to nurture that *spirituality of the ordinary* we've been discussing?

First Things First

A good place to start is to pause, catch your breath, and take a few moments to think seriously about what's *really* important to you. What means the most to you. This can serve as the North Star to tell you which way you're facing and whether you're marching in the right or the wrong direction. Your daily priorities should grow organically out of your commitment to what's most important in your life.

Go back to the exercises and questions that accompany chapter 7 and ask yourself again: *What are the most important things in my life?* Write them down. Memorize them. Carry them in your wallet or purse. Look at them several times a day. When you are trying to decide whether to do one thing or another, ask yourself which choice would serve your deepest values and which would detract from them.

Stephen Covey has an excellent discussion of this issue of balancing work with the rest of life in his book, *First Things First.*[1] We all have many roles to fill, says Covey. Too often we think of balance as an either/or process—we compartmentalize our lives among our many roles and think that balance consists of running back and forth between the different compartments.

But true balance is more holistic. It recognizes that our roles are not separate but interrelated. Rather than fragmentation, balance implies integration.

The key, says Covey, is to assure that our roles are *mission-driven,* that they emerge from the meaning and purpose of our lives. Decide what's most important and let your roles flow naturally from that. As Covey explains, "The vital factor in any choice concerning balance in our lives is a deep connection with our inner voice of conscience."

This doesn't mean that your life will always be in perfect equilibrium. Nobody's life is. Short-term imbalances are inevitable. Think of a mother taking care of her newborn child. Think of someone who quits her job to start her own business. Think of a young executive the night before her first presentation to the board of directors. These short-term imbalances, however, can contribute to long-term balance in your life. But when the short-term imbalance becomes long-term, or when the imbalance detracts from your deepest values, then you should reexamine whether you're really putting first things first.

My Life in (and out of) Balance

This talk about balance might strike you as hopelessly abstract. Let me bring it down to earth. There are times when I feel that my life is out of balance. There are times when I fear that I'm investing too much of myself in my work and not enough in everything else.

One example dates from my first year as an associate in a large law firm. Everything was new and intimidating. I was constantly trying to prove myself—everyday was a new challenge, a new obstacle to overcome, a new chance to succeed or fail. I took the first train to work in the morning and the last train home at night. Even when I was at home on evenings and weekends, I was either working or worrying about work. Clearly, my life was out of kilter.

There were a few things that helped to restore my sense of equilibrium. The first was to make a conscious effort to spend time with my wife. In the beginning, I resisted when my wife would plead, cajole, and sometimes push me out the door of our apartment so that we could spend a few hours watching a movie or going to dinner. Eventually, I realized how important this time was. It strengthened our relationship by keeping the lines of communication open between us. Not only that, it also made me a *better* worker by giving my anxious mind a much needed rest.

A second source of balance came from getting together with other people who were facing similar pressures at work. Two or three times a month I would meet with a few friends from law school who were working in other firms around town. Our get-togethers were combination lunches and b.s. sessions. These meetings did wonders for my perspective. I found myself becoming less anxious and self-absorbed as I discovered that my friends were dealing with the same worries and concerns I was facing. We helped ourselves by helping each other.

Another thing that helped was to take ten or fifteen minutes during my morning commute to sit quietly, reflect about my life, and say a few prayers. This helped center me for the day. It gave me a sense of perspective. It allowed me to see the ways in which my work was an integral part of my spiritual life. (I'll have more to say in the next chapter about carving out time for prayer and meditation.)

Together, these small things helped bring my life and my work back into balance. They let me see my work more realistically. They stopped me from investing too much of myself in my work. And they reminded me that I was more than a worker and that my work was only work.

Work as Play

I've discovered something else, too: If I want to keep my work in balance, it's important to have some fun with it.

I grew up the oldest son in a hard-working family. Responsibility, commitment, discipline—these words come easily to me. But fun, relaxation, doing nothing, goofing off—these have always had the faint waft of sin around them, as if once I surrendered to their illicit seductions I might never be able to resist. I have learned, though, that all work and no play does make you dull—and it also makes you cranky, tense, and a pain-in-the-neck to be around.

I now try to make my work a little less somber and a little more playful. I try to laugh when I find myself taking my work or myself too seriously. I remind myself that I can't do everything perfectly and shouldn't even try. I think it was G. K. Chesterton who said that anything worth doing is worth doing poorly. If something is important enough to do, then it must be worth doing, even if I can only do it poorly, not perfectly.

Each day I ask myself: How can I see my work more as a fascinating game, and less as a grim task that I must do and must do perfectly? How can I lighten up, loosen up?

I've also brought some odds and ends into my office to remind me that work isn't the only thing in my life. As I write this page, I can look up and see pictures of my wife and children, some *Star Trek* toys my sons gave me for Christmas, a poster that exclaims (truthfully), "Everyone Should Be Italian at Least Once a Year," a framed print of a wolf in a shadowy forest, and a calendar that offers a full 365 days of pictures and gossip about Frank Sinatra.

I also keep some items near me that have spiritual significance. An icon from a Russian monastery, the Prayer of St. Francis, a picture of Gandhi spinning at a loom, a tiny figurine of a laughing Buddha. My workplace is holy ground, and I don't want to forget that.

These odds and ends help keep my work in perspective. They remind me that I bring all of myself to the office. They make it easier for me to be the same person at work that I am at home.

True balance isn't a question of either/or, work or home, business or family. It's a question of finding ways to bring the two together, to embed your work in the whole of your life, so that your work becomes a bright and beautiful thread in the warp and the woof of the life you are weaving.

EXERCISES AND QUESTIONS

1. It seems like everyone wants to achieve "balance" in life. What does that mean to you? Be specific. What steps are you taking to achieve a healthy balance between your work and the rest of your life? What helps the most?

2. I suggested in this chapter that you take some time to think about and write down the two or three most important things in your life, as a way to keep "first things first." Did you do it? If not, why not? What are you waiting for? What are you afraid of?

3. Complete the following sentences:

   Three things I do for fun are...

   Three things I do for relaxation are...

   My hobbies are...

   What do your answers say about you?

4. Look back at the exercises and questions from chapter 16. Have you planted a garden, woven a quilt, played tennis, learned Spanish, gone to an opera, etc.? What are you waiting for?

5. I've asked this before, but it's worth coming back to time and again: How do you deal with the inevitable pressures and stresses of work? Have you found healthy ways to handle the pressures or do you eat too much, drink too much, etc.? Do you have good friends you can talk to about your work?

6. This one may be hard, so take your time. What are one or two things you could do to make your work a little more playful and a little less serious? (Hint: When's the last time you laughed, really laughed, when at work?).

7. What does your office or work space say about you? If a stranger entered your work space, what would he learn about you? Would he be able to detect what's most important to you? Does your work space include reminders of the persons and things you love?

THE RHYTHM OF
THE SPIRITUAL LIFE

20

If there has been one persistent theme in this book, it has been to warn against the dangers of compartmentalizing your life. I have insisted that there are no barriers between the sacred and the profane. You find the sacred right here, right now. I've argued that there's not enough time for the spiritual life if you approach it as one more thing to do, one more chore to complete.

But there's a paradox here. If you want to cultivate a spirituality of the ordinary, you probably need to take some time *away from* your ordinary life. As we've seen, it can be difficult if not impossible to appreciate the sacredness of ordinary life when you're being pushed and pulled by the pressures of work, family, and home. How can you maintain your spiritual center of balance when your life is a never-ending race from the dentist to the office to the supermarket? How can you hear the still small voice of God amidst the clamor and the clatter that fills up your day?

I can remember a period at work when I felt overwhelmed by the long hours, constant phone calls, endless meetings, and urgent deadlines. I felt myself swept away as if on a tide, like a tired swimmer being carried out to sea. Although I didn't realize it at the time, I was simultaneously treating my work as a curse and as an idol.

This continued for several months. Finally, I took a few days off and went on a retreat. Only then did I have the luxury of looking at my work and noticing where I had gone wrong. Only then did I have the time and the space to rethink my attitudes and adopt a few measures to help me take work more seriously than a curse but less seriously than an idol.

Each of us needs to find ways to bring moments of quiet reflection, meditation, prayer, and the like into our too-busy lives. As theologian Harvey Cox suggests, spirituality "is nurtured not by a single-minded withdrawal from the world but by a rhythm of advance and retreat, of wading into the pain and conflict of the secular realm, and repairing into the sustenance of solitude and a supporting community."[1] Your spirituality of work is forged in the constant give-and-take of daily life, but it's refined in occasional periods of quiet and reflection.

Daily Disengagements

I'm not suggesting that you embark on a pilgrimage to a distant land or spend a month in silent retreat at a Buddhist temple or a Catholic monastery (although for some people, that would be fine). In my life, what helps most are short periods of reflection during the day and longer periods of quiet once or twice a year.

During my usual workday, I try to do a few simple things to provide a measure of reflection. I often spend a few minutes in the morning reading Scripture or a book with a spiritual message. I find that even if I read for only ten minutes or so, usually at the coffee shop near my office, it helps me ease into the day, like wading into the shallow end of a pool before diving in. I often find that the themes I'm reading about—this morning, for example, I was reading an essay about the need for patience in the spiritual life—set the stage for my day. My reading helps focus my attention during the workday, so that I become particularly aware of certain things and open to certain experiences.

At other times, I spend ten or fifteen minutes in silence. I relax, clear my head of thoughts, and pay attention to my breathing, in and out, in and out. As thoughts (often about work) push their way into my head, I notice them, gently dismiss them, and return to the gentle in-and-out of my breathing. I am no expert at meditation, but even those few minutes leave me with a sense of calmness and energy that stays with me throughout the day.

I find the experience more rewarding if I also do a little writing. I have never been successful at keeping a journal for long periods of time—I start strong but fade away after a few weeks. Instead, I make a few notes about my reading, my reflections, or my dreams (recall the discussion of dreams in chapter 14). Sometimes I draw a few tentative connections between what I've just experienced and what (I suspect) awaits me at work and at home. If I read a passage about the importance of trusting my intuition, I might think about a meeting I've scheduled for later that day, and vow not to overprepare but to trust my inner voice to guide me. I usually end my session with a few moments of prayer.

When I'm at work, I try to find a few minutes here and there to catch my breath and take stock of the day. I often have meetings at various locations on my college campus, and rather than drive, I usually walk, which gives me a few minutes of quiet time and exercise. Sometimes I stop for a few minutes of prayer at a church that's near my office. If I have to run an errand at lunch, I may turn off the car radio and use the fifteen minutes of silence as a miniretreat. Occasionally, I take the phone off the hook for a few minutes to gather my thoughts. Sometimes, when I'm especially busy, I may not have time to do anything but stretch my legs by walking the long way around when I go to pick up my mail or buy a soda.

What works best for me is to fit these few minutes of prayer and reflection into my daily routine. If I try to add reflection time to my already full plate of activities, it becomes one more obligation, one more thing to do. But if I can combine a short reflection period with something I have to do anyway—walk across campus or drive across town—then it becomes less of a burden and more of a respite from my burdens.

Retreating from Work

I also find it helpful to take a few days once or twice a year and escape the nonstop pace of home and office. Usually I go to a retreat house near the city in which I live, although occasionally I housesit for a friend who lives on the other side of town. I bring along some reading, spiritual and otherwise, some music, maybe a book on tape, and a journal.

I spend most of the first day sleeping, a clear message from my body about the fatigue and tension I carry all the time without being conscious of it. I take long walks. I debrief the last few months and reflect about what's been happening in my life: What challenges and problems have I encountered? What has gone well and what has gone badly in my relationships with family, friends, and others? How have I treated those I love the most?

I also assess my spiritual life: How have I responded to the deep urgings of the spirit? Have I been living soulfully or soullessly? Have my daily responsibilities and pressures squeezed God out of the picture?

I take some time to reflect about the ways I have been approaching my work: Have I been treating my work as a curse? As an idol? Have I nurtured a sense of calling in my work? I try to be specific: At what times, and under what circumstances, have I gravitated toward one or another of these images of work? Have I taken advantage of the opportunities in my work for ministry, service, and a spirituality of the ordinary? How have I balanced my work with the rest of my life?

I look ahead as well. I usually bring my appointment calendar and look at the next few months. I try to arrange my schedule to make time for myself and my family. I may pencil into the calendar certain times to have lunch with friends or to attend a special talk, liturgy, or concert.

I commit myself to one or two things that I will focus on during the next few months—a mini–New

Year's resolution without the pressure. I might resolve to spend ten minutes each morning in meditation or to make sure that my wife and I reserve a few hours each week to spend with each other without kids or interruptions.

I also spend some time probing the moral dimensions of my work: Do I have my priorities right? How have I treated colleagues, clients, bosses, and the other people I've met? Have I been faithful, respectful, compassionate? What problems have I encountered in my moral life? What tough decisions have I been putting off? Have I handled the little things at work in a way that will give me the moral reserves to handle any big things that might arise?

It was in such a period of quiet reflection that I finally came to the conclusion that I was being called to leave the practice of law and become a teacher. It was at another time of retreat that I summoned up the courage to quit a comfortable job and enter the strange new world of the seminary. It was during such a time that I made a pledge—not always honored, but never forgotten—to spend a few hours each week alone with each of my children. So many of the most important decisions in my life would never have been made without these periods of prayer and reflection.

Do Something Instead of Nothing

The form that your retreat might take is entirely up to you. Some people, like myself, gravitate toward solitude because of our personality or because of the demands of our daily life. Some people enjoy going on a formal retreat at a monastery or retreat house. Others like to go camping for a few days.

For some people, the thought of taking two or three days off is daunting. How will I fill up the time? What will I do with myself? If you feel that way, the answer is to *think small.* Your retreat might consist of nothing more elaborate than taking the phone off the hook for a few hours or spending a day planting in your garden, walking in the woods, or sitting on your back porch sipping iced tea and enjoying the sun.

Too much solitude, of course, can turn into spiritual navel gazing. Recall Harvey Cox's suggestion that we repair regularly into solitude *and a supporting community.* Don't think that the discipline of reflection must be done alone. My wife goes away with a few girlfriends for a long weekend once a year—they spend the time talking, laughing, and sometimes crying. For some people, attendance at church services is their chief spiritual sustenance. Many people participate in a variety of other activities at their church, synagogue, or mosque—adult study programs, scripture groups, retreats, and the like.

As is so often the case with the spiritual life, the specifics of what you do are not what's most important—what's most important is that you do *something* rather than nothing. The precise format has to fit your own lifestyle and personality. Do whatever it takes to carve out occasional periods of disengagement in the midst of your hectic life. Each of us has a spirituality of work, even if it's unconscious and inarticulate, but we may continue for years as the captive of our unconscious images and assumptions unless we make the time to step back and examine what we've taken for granted.

The spiritual life is a rhythm of advance and retreat, advance and retreat. Only if you occasionally retreat will you be able to see what you've been advancing toward. Only with some distance from your work can you appreciate how *little* distance exists between your work and your spiritual life.

EXERCISES AND QUESTIONS

1. How do you carve out space for yourself in the midst of your busy life? Do you take the time you need?

2. What spiritual practices do you build into your day? What spiritual practices have you wanted to try but keep putting off because you haven't had the time? Could you find the time if you really tried?

3. Do this for a month: Take ten or fifteen minutes for yourself in the morning. Take the phone off the hook. Lock the door if you have to. This is your time, nobody else's.

   During your private time, sit quietly. Read a spiritual book, if you want to. Meditate on your breath. Listen to soft music and let your mind wander. Get out of your chair and practice yoga or Tai Chi. Reflect on your dreams. Do whatever you want (as long as you stay awake).

   When you're done, jot down a line or two in a notebook to serve as your "spiritual compass" for the day. Take these few words with you. Come back to them several times during the day.

4. Consider taking a few days off from work and making a retreat. You can find the location of nearby retreat houses by talking to a local priest, minister, or rabbi.

   If the idea of a retreat sounds scary, start small. Try taking your phone off the hook for a few hours and making a miniretreat at home.

5. With all the pressures of modern life, it's easy to forget how fortunate we are. Take a sheet of paper and write down the things you're grateful for:

I am grateful for...

Don't stop until you've filled up an entire sheet of paper. Include big things (family, health, religion, etc.) and little things (that new CD you bought last week, that bird outside your window, etc.). Whenever you find yourself forgetting the good things in your life, take out another sheet of paper and fill it up.

6. Now that we're near the end of this book, it's time to ask: How many of the exercises and questions did you do? Which exercises and questions were most helpful? Which are worth coming back to in the future?

Did you feel a strong resistance to certain exercises and questions—if so, did you do them anyway?

Go back over the book quickly and review any passages that particularly challenged you, pleased you, comforted you, upset you, angered you, etc. What do your responses to these passages tell you about yourself and your work?

Now ask yourself: What are one or two things that you can take from this book and continue to use after you've finished reading it? Maybe it's one idea, one exercise or question. Whatever it is, how will you make it part of your life?

7. I said at the beginning of this book that I saw it as a conversation between us. But in another sense,

it has been an opportunity for you to have a conversation with yourself. You've been reflecting about your own life. You've been asking yourself questions. You've been challenging yourself. You've been helping yourself.

Now that this book is ending, I wonder: *How will you keep this conversation going?*

EPILOGUE: THE SPIRIT AT WORK

Life plays tricks on us all. In the midst of writing this book, I found myself dealing with a series of nagging problems at work. Most were beyond my capacity to control, but that didn't make them any easier to endure. I was anxious and tense. I slept badly. I lost my temper and my equilibrium.

When everything is going well, it seems so easy to cultivate a spirituality of work. When things are going well, you feel refreshed and invigorated by your work. You find purpose, meaning, and creativity in everything you do. You instinctively approach your work as a calling and sense God's presence all around you.

The real test of a spirituality of work comes when things aren't going well, when you encounter disappointment and frustration, when joy dries up and meaning disappears. That's the place I found myself when writing this book.

My first thought was to put down the project altogether. I felt like a fraud, a hypocrite, writing about the spirituality of work when my own work was sterile and unrewarding. How dare I presume to talk about the *spirit at work* when I couldn't find the spirit in my own work!

I stopped writing. I went to work, taught my classes, met with students, attended meetings, but it was dry as ashes. All I could do was get up each day, go to work, do my best—and wait, hope, and pray.

One morning I came to work and was met at my office door by a student. "I just came to say thanks," she told me.

It took me a moment to remember her. A few weeks before she had come to my office to discuss a course I was teaching. During this conversation, she had told me that she was thinking about quitting law school. I had been so preoccupied with my own worries that I had given her little attention or sympathy. I had sat half-listening, half-caring, as she told me of her feelings of inadequacy. Finally, her words had run out and we had sat in an uncomfortable silence for what seemed an eternity—but was probably only a minute. Then she had picked up her things and left.

It was not my finest hour. Now that I remembered how cold and unfeeling I had been, I couldn't help but laugh nervously. "Thanks for what? I didn't do anything."

"Just for listening," she said. "I feel a lot better since we talked." She smiled, and I smiled back, feeling so much better about my work and my life. When she left, I sat down and started writing again for the first time in weeks.

*   *   *

The spiritual life comes with no guarantees. One day you're overwhelmed by the beauty of the world. God is everywhere. You can feel and taste the sanctity of creation. Your work is good; your life is complete.

Another day and everything changes. You find no joy in your life, no beauty in the world. God has fled and you are left alone.

Things go well, things go badly. You take a step forward, you take a step backward. You can never be sure what's waiting for you around the next bend in the road. Wonder and dread beckon. All you know for certain is that the journey is worth taking, must be taken, if you're going to be truly human, truly alive.

The heart has its reasons. The soul resists being catalogued, summarized, or contained. There's a mystery about the spiritual life that can never be explained away.

Words like *calling* or *vocation* can be helpful to anyone who wants to nurture purpose and meaning at work. Words like *creativity* and *love* and *service* are useful reminders of what's really important in our life and in our work. Words like *curse* and *idol* can function as warning signs on our spiritual journey.

But they're only words. We can't help but use words when we think and talk about the spiritual life, but words can't help but fall short of reality. In the end, all of our talk about *soul* and *spirit* is only a feeble attempt to make some sense of the unchartable realms of the ineffable.

The spirit blows where it will. Our job—our life's work—is not to direct or dominate the spirit, but to listen, watch, wait, and respond. That seems so little, but it's enough. It's everything, really.

We're not in control; the spirit is. At our meetings and offices, assembly lines and factories; while we drive our trucks and write our memos, send our faxes and fold our clothes; at home or at work, with family or friends, customers or colleagues; awake or asleep; yesterday, today, and tomorrow—wherever we are, whatever we do, the spirit is present, the spirit is moving, the spirit is working.

The more you open yourself to the spirit, and answer the spirit's call, the easier it will become to love what you do and do what you love. Enthusiasm and excitement will follow. If you love your job, you'll find your passion.

NOTES

INTRODUCTION

1. See especially the works of Thomas Moore, such as *Care of the Soul: A Guide for Cultivating Depth and Sacredness in Everyday Life* (New York: HarperCollins, 1992); *Soul Mates: Honoring the Mysteries of Love and Relationship* (New York: HarperCollins, 1994); and *The Re-Enchantment of Everyday Life* (New York: HarperCollins, 1996).

3. WHEN WORK IS A JOB

1. Frederick Buechner, *Listening to Your Life: Daily Meditations with Frederick Buechner* (New York: HarperCollins, 1992), p. 54.
2. Studs Terkel, *Working: People Talk About What They Do All Day and How They Feel About Doing It* (New York: Ballantine Books, 1985), pp. xiii–xiv.

4. CURSED BE THE GROUND

1. Studs Terkel, *Working: People Talk About What They Do All Day and How They Feel About What They Do* (New York: Ballantine Books, 1985), p. xiii.
2. Genesis 3:17–19 (New Jewish Publication Society Translation).

5. CLIMBING THE LADDER OF SUCCESS

1. Robert N. Bellah, Richard Madsen, William M. Sullivan, Ann Swidler, Steven M. Tipton, *Habits of the Heart: Individualism and Commitment in American Life* (New York: Harper & Row, 1985), p. 66.

6. WHAT WORK PROFESSES

1. There is a good overview of the development of the professions by Stephen F. Barker: "What Is a Profession?"in *Professional Ethics*, vol. 1, 1992, pp. 73–99.

7. THE GOD WHO CAN'T SAVE

1. James E. Dittes, *When Work Goes Sour* (Philadelphia: Westminster Press, 1987), p. 7.
2. James Luther Adams, *The Prophethood of All Believers*, edited by George K. Beach (Boston: Beacon Press, 1986), p. 152.

8. THE CALL OF WORK

1. Charles Kammer, "Vocation and the Professions," in Thomas W. Ogletree, editor, *The Annual of the Society of Christian Ethics,* 1981, p. 170.
2. Michael Novak, *Business As a Calling: Work and the Examined Life* (New York: The Free Press, 1996), p. 18.

9. HEARING THE CALL

1. Michael Novak, *Business As a Calling: Work and the Examined Life* (New York: The Free Press, 1996), pp. 34–36.

2. A helpful resource for exploring the relationship between your personality and your work is Paul D. Tieger and Barbara Barron-Tieger's *Do What You Are: Discover the Perfect Career for You Through the Secrets of Personality Type* (New York: Little-Brown and Company, 2d ed. 1995).

3. Frederick Buechner, *Listening to Your Life: Daily Meditations with Frederick Buechner* (New York: HarperCollins, 1992), pp. 185–86.

10. LIVING THE SILENCE

1. E. F. Schumacher, *Good Work* (New York: Harper & Row, 1979), p. 118.

13. TAKING OFF THE MASKS

1. The quotations from Jung in this chapter are from C. G. Jung, *The Archetypes and the Collective Unconscious* (Princeton, N.J.: Princeton University Press, 2d ed., 1968), pp. 122-123.

2. Quoted in Thomas L. Shaffer and James R. Elkins, *Legal Interviewing and Counseling, (St. Paul, Minn.:* West Publishing Group, 3d edition, 1997), pp. 4–5. My discussion of the persona owes much to Shaffer and Elkins.

3. George Orwell's reflections on the masks we wear appear in his brilliant essay, "Shooting an

Elephant," which was written in 1936 and has been reprinted many times since. See, for example, George Orwell, *Shooting an Elephant and Other Essays* (New York: Harcourt, Brace & World, Inc., 1950), pp. 3–12.

4. *The Essential Jung*, selected and introduced by Anthony Storr (Princeton, N.J.: Princeton University Press, 1983), p. 87.

14. DREAMS OF WORK

1. Thomas Moore, *The Re-Enchantment of Everyday Life* (New York: HarperCollins, 1996), p. 360.

15. EROS AT WORK

1. Quoted in Matthew Fox, *The Reinvention of Work: A New Vision of Livelihood for Our Time* (New York: HarperCollins, 1994), p. 307.

2. Thomas Moore, *The Re-Enchantment of Everyday Life* (New York: HarperCollins, 1996), p. 132. The two subsequent quotations from Moore are found at pages 131 and 133.

16. HONORING YOUR CREATIVITY

1. Quoted in Julia Cameron, *The Artist's Way: A Spiritual Path to Higher Creativity* (New York: Tarcher/Putnam, 1992), p. 2. The quote from Shakti Gawain later in this chapter appears in Cameron, p. 63.

2. Quoted in Matthew Fox, *The Reinvention of Work: A New Vision of Livelihood for Our Time* (New York: HarperCollins, 1994), p. 117.

3. M. C. Richards, *Centering in Pottery, Poetry, and the Person* (Middletown, Conn.: Wesleyan University Press, 1962), p. 12. The subsequent quotation from Richards is on p. 27.

17. LOVE MADE VISIBLE

1. Martin Buber, *I and Thou* (New York: Charles Scribner's Sons, 2d edition, 1958), p. 18.

2. Frederick Buechner, *Listening to Your Life: Daily Meditations with Frederick Buechner* (New York: HarperCollins, 1992), pp. 185–86.

3. William L. Droel, *The Spirituality of Work: Lawyers* (Chicago: National Center for the Laity, 1989), p. 38.

4. Quoted in Jack Canfield and Jacqueline Miller, *Heart at Work: Stories and Strategies for Building Self-Esteem and Reawakening the Soul at Work* (New York: McGraw-Hill, 1996), p. 36.

18. PRACTICING WHAT YOU PREACH

1. Thomas V. Morris, *Legal Ethics in an Unethical World* (transcript of a videotape series) (Notre Dame, Ind.: The National Institute for Trial Advocacy, 1992), p. 24.

2. Harper Lee, *To Kill a Mockingbird* (New York: Warner Books [Paperback edition], 1982), p. 34.

3. Many spiritual writers have made this point. A recent example is found in Richard Carlson's pop-

ular book, *Don't Sweat the Small Stuff...and It's All Small Stuff* (New York: Hyperion, 1997). One of the chapters in Carlson's book is entitled "Remember that You Become What You Practice Most."

19. BALANCING THE WORK OF A LIFE

1. Stephen R. Covey, A. Roger Merrill, Rebecca A. Merrill, *First Things First: To Live, To Love, To Learn, To Leave a Legacy* (New York: Simon & Schuster, 1994). The subsequent quotation from Covey is on p. 127.

20. THE RHYTHM OF THE SPIRITUAL LIFE

1. Harvey Cox, *Religion in the Secular City: Toward a Modern Theology* (New York: Simon and Schuster, 1984), p. 210.

BIBLIOGRAPHY

The following resources have proven especially helpful to my thinking about the relationship between spirituality and work.

Allegretti, Joseph G. *The Lawyer's Calling: Christian Faith and Legal Practice*. Mahwah, N.J.: Paulist Press, 1996.

Banks, Robert. *God the Worker: Journeys into the Mind, Heart, and Imagination of God*. Valley Forge, Penna.: Judson Press, 1992.

Bellah, Robert N., Richard Madsen, William M. Sullivan, Ann Swidler, and Steven M. Tipton. *Habits of the Heart: Individualism and Commitment in American Life*. New York: Harper & Row, 1985.

Buechner, Frederick. *Listening to Your Life: Daily Meditations with Frederick Buechner*. New York: Harper-Collins, 1992.

Cameron, Julia. *The Artist's Way: A Spiritual Path to Higher Creativity*. New York: Tarcher/Putnam, 1992.

Canfield, Jack, and Jacqueline Miller. *Heart at Work: Stories and Strategies for Building Self-Esteem and Reawakening the Soul at Work*. New York: McGraw Hill, 1996.

Covey, Stephen R., A. Roger Merrill, and Rebecca R. Merrill. *First Things First: To Live, To Love, To Learn, To Leave a Legacy*. New York: Simon & Schuster, 1994.

Diehl, William E. *The Monday Connection: A Spirituality of Competence, Affirmation, and Support in the Workplace*. New York: HarperCollins, 1991.

Dittes, James E. *When Work Goes Sour*. Philadelphia: Westminster Press, 1987.

Fox, Matthew. *The Reinvention of Work: A New Vision of Livelihood for Our Time*. New York: HarperCollins, 1994.

Goosen, Gideon. *The Theology of Work*. Hales Corners, Wis.: Clergy Book Service, no date.

Hardy, Lee. *The Fabric of This World: Inquiries into Calling, Career Choice, and the Design of Human Work*. Grand Rapids, Mich.: Eerdmans, 1990.

Haughey, John C. *Converting Nine to Five: A Spirituality of Daily Work*. New York: Crossroad, 1989.

Holloway, James Y., and Will D. Campbell. *Callings!* New York: Paulist Press, 1974.

Initiatives. A newsletter devoted to exploring the connections between faith and work. Available from the National Center for the Laity, P.O. Box 291102, Chicago, Ill., 60629.

Kinast, Robert L. *Work: An Adult Discussion Program*. Part of the Vatican II: Act II Series. Collegeville, Minn.: Liturgical Press, 1995.

Moore, Thomas. *The Re-Enchantment of Everyday Life*. New York: HarperCollins, 1996.

Mount, Eric, Jr. *Professional Ethics in Context: Institutions, Images, and Empathy*. Louisville, Ken.: Westminster/John Knox Press, 1990.

National Conference of Catholic Bishops. *Economic Justice for All: Pastoral Letter on Catholic Social Teaching and the U.S. Economy*. Washington, D.C.: United States Catholic Conference, 1986.

Novak, Michael. *Business as a Calling: Work and the Examined Life*. New York: The Free Press, 1996.

On Human Work: A Resource Book for the Study of Pope John II's Third Encyclical. Washington, D.C.: United States Catholic Conference, 1982.

Palmer, Parker J. *The Active Life: Wisdom for Work, Creativity, and Caring.* New York: HarperCollins, 1991.

Pierce, Gregory F. Augustine, ed. *Of Human Hands: A Reader in the Spirituality of Work.* Minneapolis, Minn.: Augsburg, 1991.

Raines, John C., and Donna C. Day-Lower. *Modern Work and Human Meaning.* Philadelphia: Westminster, 1986.

Richardson, Alan. *The Biblical Doctrine of Work.* London: SCM Press, 1963.

Richards, M. C. *Centering in Pottery, Poetry, and the Person.* Middletown, Conn.: Wesleyan University Press, 1964.

Schor, Juliet B. *The Overworked American: The Unexpected Decline of Leisure.* New York: HarperCollins, 1991.

Schumacher, E. F. *Good Work.* New York: Harper & Row, 1979.

Soelle, Dorothy, and Shirley A. Cloyes. *To Work and to Love: A Theology of Creation.* Philadelphia: Fortress Press, 1984.

Steere, Douglas V. *Work and Contemplation.* New York: Harper & Brothers, 1957.

Terkel, Studs. *Working: People Talk About What They Do All Day and How They Feel About What They Do.* New York: Ballantine Books, 1985.

Tieger, Paul D., and Barbara Barron-Tieger, *Do What You Are: Discover the Perfect Career for You Through the Secrets of Personality Type.* New York: Little, Brown and Company, 2d edition, 1995.

Williams, Oliver F., and John W. Houck. *Full Value: Cases in Christian Business Ethics*. San Francisco: Harper & Row, 1978.

Whyte, David. *The Heart Aroused: Poetry and the Preservation of the Soul in Corporate America*. New York: Doubleday, 1994.

Also helpful is a series of pamphlets from ACTA Publications. "The Spirituality of Work" series includes volumes on *Nurses, Teachers, Lawyers, Homemakers, Unemployed Workers*, and others.